FRUITCAKE

J. Beresford Hines

Relentless Publishing House, LLC
Columbia, SC

FruitCake

Published by :

Relentless Publishing House, LLC

ISBN: 9781948829946

First Edition: Noember 2019

10 9 8 7 6 5 4 3 2 1

FruitCake

In a youth-centered society, now comes a comedy about a family views on the elderly. FruitCake follows the family challenges of acceptance of older family members residing in their homes, life and their comfort zones.

EXT. BELAIR FUNERAL HOME-DAY

A sign reads, "Closing due to bankruptcy," covering the word funeral and just exposing the name Belair home. Adjacent to the funeral home is the New Belair rest home for seniors. The doors are open and people move in and out. A black Coroner's van parks outside the funeral office.

INT. DAY FUNERAL HOME OFFICE-SEMI-LIT

Twin brother and sister FERN and DERN have identical black Coroner's jackets on. Their names are on their jackets. They are cleaning out the offices of paper work and items.

Fern is at the vault and Dern is behind her with a flashlight. She opens it and the sound of metal against metal is heard. Dern flashes the light quickly on the objects inside but accidently pops Fern in the head. She jabs her elbow into his gut, which drops him, as she grabs the flashlight on his way down.

Fern pans down the vault shelves with the flashlight. Dern from the floor pushes away cobwebs. Several urns are present and labeled by its cremation year. They are also tagged as occupied and unoccupied.

The cremation dates reading downward begin with the year 2009. Fern and Dern look at each other and starting one by one shaking urns. Some of the urns spilled and they begin trying to place some of the dust back inside. Fern sneezes dust on Dern. He bumps his head on a shelf and nearly knocks over all of the urns.

Fern grabs her brother and steadies him, while he holds her nose so she won't sneeze any more. They both notice only one name and undisturbed urn survived them. The year of cremation reads 1999 occupied and the name is Walter Gillespie.

FERN
Call!

DERN
You call.

FERN
I phoned last time when we were locked in the body-bags. We had the cells.

DERN
The boss didn't laugh when we sat up.

FERN
Boss must have peed himself when he got a call from the body-bag.

DERN
We need this job. Mom and daddy will kick us out. Ask the boss about the 1999 dust dude.

Fern walks over to the desk and slightly looses her balance on the urn dust then straightens herself.

DERN
You're a lady. . .

Dern chuckles and eases away from the fault. Then stands in front of the desk. Fern finds the number and calls on the speaker.

FERN
Hello Billy this is . . .

BILLY

I know who this is. It's Sud and Dud and I told you two, call me Bill-Lee not Billy! What do you want?

FERN

We found a jar that's been here since 1999. What do you want us to do with it?

BILLY

Look soapy and soupy. All I told you guys to do was close that place down. We only have a week. Call his people to come get him. Call them, not me. Just close the place down!

There is a loud dial tone and Fern looks at Dern.

FERN

Your turn to call. What's the guy's name?

Dern fingers the Walter Gillespie nameplate but hesitates speaking, sputtering. Fern is right behind him.

FERN

I told ma, I was a better speller. Those twelve years in elementary did me fine. You make the calls.

Dern replaces Fern at the desk and Fern calls out the letters. She hurls a phone book at her brother.

FERN

Look it up in the picture book. It will show you how to say stuff.

Dern looks at the phone-book, then at his sister but ignores her. Fern calls out the letters slowly, Gi-ll-es-pie.

FERN

G-i-ll-es-pie.

DERN

Its Gil-les-pie. You should say the last part like apple pie. The first part like jills, like our cousins Jack and Jill.

FERN

That's not it. It's like the gill on a fish and les like in, not more and pie like, ah yeah you right. You see any of his people in that book?

DERN

A shovel full of people.

FERN

Start calling. I'll get lunch.

Dern calls as Fern again slips on cremation dust as she exits.

INT. Restaurant Kitchen-Midday

BROTHER shouting out orders to frantic cooks and waiters. In a madhouse deli kitchen, he glances at the kitchen clock and shakes his head at 12 PM. The phone rings and he takes down the order. He unwraps his apron and washes his hands.

BROTHER
OK day-shift, the last of night shift is through, it's all on you.

There is a boo from the crew as Brother puts on his jacket which reads Brother's home repair and he smiles and exits.

I/E. BROTHER'S PICKUP TRUCK

Brother checks his clipboard of scheduled visits. He drives away from a full parking lot of lunch patrons at a twenty-four hour deli.

INT/EXT. PICKUP TRUCK-MOMENTS LATER

Brother looks for a newly renovated house. He pulls into the driveway and exits his truck grabbing his tools. Several men are putting in electrical wiring, and constructing the house as Brother enters.

FOREMAN
The rookie, thanks for joining us. The job starts a 12.

BROTHER
Sorry, I had to get off ... You don't want to hear that.

FOREMAN
You're right! Get to work. We're behind so get it.

Foreman walks away looking at others work and complaining. He shouts back at Brother.

FOREMAN

When will you be finish plumbing school princess?

BROTHER

School will be finished soon.

Sarcastically, foreman tries to get last word in.

FOREMAN

Yeah right. How long is soon?

Brother reluctantly ignores him.

INT.FUNERAL HOME OFFICE-DAY

DERN

There's a lot of Gil-les-pies in this fat book.

He's continually turning pages reading up and down.

FERN

You've got to hurry. Stop looking at the pictures. Make some more calls.

Dern begins dialing then speaks.

DERN

Most of them have those boxes that talk back to you. They're telling me ain't nobody home. I just let it ring,

then I figure
nobody was home.

Dern has the phone to his ear and not listening because he has made earlier calls. Fern is eating chicken wings and picking her feet. Someone on the other end picks up the phone Surprised, Dern nearly falls out of his chair and it frightens Fern as she darts for the exit door looking at the caskets and urns while grabbing her lunch.

INT. BROTHER'S HOME/DAY

Brother's teen daughter TIA is madly texting and the landline phone rings. She reluctantly picks it up and places it on her shoulder and ear. Tia keeps texting with both hands. She answers quick and abrupt.

TIA
Gillespie-
residents-do-you-
want-to-leave-a-
message?

Surprised by the quick questions, Dern is unable to get out all the message.

DERN
Oh! Huh? Ah Mr.
Gil-les-pie this is
Dern and my sister
Fern. .

He is interrupted by Tia because of the way he pronounced the last name.

TIA
Excuse me? Who are
you looking for?

Dern is flustered. He motions the phone to Fern but she refuses while cutting her toe nails and eating the hot chicken wings.

DERN

We're from Belair
and we've got your
people and his
stuff here. Pick
him up by fish day-
come weeks-end!
Have a nice day-
dinner, Walter's
his name.

He hangs up gasping, grabs a chicken wing, and taps Fern's wing like toasting glasses. Dern leans back, his feet on the desk and hands behind his head revealing his sweating armpits. Tia hangs up, shrugs and continues her texting.

I/E. BROTHER'S PICKUP TRUCK/EVENING

Brother in his driveway, signs some papers and multi-tasks his truck-office.

INT. BROTHER'S HOME-EVENING MOMENTS LATER

He comes through the side door moving randomly while kissing his wife MARIA and rubs the head of Tia who is still texting in the kitchen, doing homework and helping her mom.

MARIA

Honey, I know you
have to go but I
need you to pick up
the kids.

Brother changes jackets and into a collared shirt.

BROTHER

Maria, you know I'm
on my way to class?

Maria looks at Brother as he darts in and out of different rooms looking for something. She holds out his books as he sees them. He takes them and nods a thank you and winks.

BROTHER
OK, but when I come back, I'm not coming in. Have Tia meet me outside! I can't miss this plumbing class. Any repair customers calls?

MARIA
No, not since I've been home, Tia?

They tap her on her shoulder because she's listening to music. Maria motions with her mouth. (Have there been any calls for daddy?) Tia motions her head no. Brother is dressed and kissing his ladies and exiting. Tia jumps, and grabs her dad. He looks around startled.

TIA
Oh daddy! Somebody did call. I couldn't understand what he was saying he sounded weird.

BROTHER
Did he have an accent?

TIA
Yes sir, he sound like he was from Staten Island.

Brother and Maria look at each other and wave their hands over their head indicating their daughter is an airhead. Brother checks the phone's previous numbers.

BROTHER

What was the message?

TIA

You're suppose to pickup somebody from Belair by the weekend. I think his name is Walter.

Brother looks at the phone hangs up.

BROTHER

I'll check it out between classes, I know Belair nursing home. We set up the plumbing there.

MARIA

Honey, the kids?

Brother heads out the door, jumps in the family car and zooms out the driveway.

I/E. BELAIR NURSING HOME EARLY LATER EVENING

Brother hesitantly walks toward the Nursing home. Music is playing and Brother watches a family returning a resident and her walker, toilet, medicines, heater and a wheel chair. Brother observes another resident arguing and hitting her son with her purse. A family is urging their mom to go inside the home but she is crying frantically and won't go inside. Brother witnesses another senior screaming at her family as they spin out of the parking lot.

Brother slows his pace and stops at the main door. He pushes on the door and pushes hard, then harder and the door does not budge. He places his shoulder against the door and shoves more. He stops and look at the door and sign on the opposite door says please use this door. He enters the Nursing home.

INT.NURSING HOME-DAY-MOMENTS-LATER.

Brother stands at the front desk. Sixties music is playing and the seniors are in an activity room. Some are sitting in chairs stoic. One resident passes Brother without him knowing it and lightly touches his jacket. It startles him and the resident keeps walking away still looking at him and not watching where they are going but doesn't bump into anything. When Brother turns to face the front, the desk clerk is directly in front of him, Brother does a double-take at how quickly she appeared. She has a name tag which says RONNIE on it.

RONNIE
Hi, can I help you?

Brother steps back because she's a close talker and he reaches in his pocket and inserts a tic-tac in his mouth and offers her some but she refuses. Brother takes another step back.

BROTHER
Yes, we received a call about a possible family member being here and he needed to be picked up?

Ronnie begins assembling a group pages and a clipboard and pen.

RONNIE
Who called?

BROTHER
Someone from Belair.

RONNIE
And you're here to pick them up?

BROTHER

No, I want to find
out why he's
leaving.

Brother is looking around the room. He's
checks his watch and taps his feet. Ronnie
starts to take notes.

BROTHER
You're writing this
down?

BROTHER
Our policy is to
document everything
that happens on our
shift.

RONNIE
What's your family
member's name?

BROTHER
Walter.

RONNIE
Oh, Walter.

BROTHER
You know him?

RONNIE
No. What's Walter's
social security
number and how long
has he been here?

BROTHER
I don't know.

RONNIE
You don't know his
client number!

Brother taps the desk. Ronnie looks at
Brother and she stops. Then checks her watch
again.

BROTHER

Gillespie is his last name, but I don't know how long he's been here.

RONNIE
When did you bring him in?

BROTHER
I don't know that either.

Ronnie shifts to the file cabinet and shuffles through and pulls out some forms. She places them on the clipboard and hands them to Brother.

RONNIE
I'll need a copy of your drivers license, and two other picture identification, and some kind of information that says you are related to our clients. I need you to initial and sign the top and bottom front and back of each form.

Brother takes clipboard, backs away from the counter and sits in a chair next to a senior sitting in a wheel chair snoozing. The gentleman looks at him. He speaks to Brother beyond earshot of Ronnie.

WHEELCHAIR WILLE
I know you, do you know me?

Brother shakes his head no.

WHEELCHAIR WILLE
You know you?

Brother shakes his head yes, as he looks around at little embarrassed he's whispering.

WHEELCHAIR WILLE

I know you. I use to have hair like you.

Wheelchair Willie rubs his own balding head.

WHEELCHAIR WILLE

Are you scared?

Brother shakes his head no.

WHEELCHAIR WILLE

I'm scared. Are you scared?

Brother shakes his head yes. Brother shyly slides his chair over, and Wheelchair Willie nods again. Brother speaks to himself out loud.

BROTHER

Lord, I need some help.

Brother looks across the hall into a large room. Seniors are talking and dancing and having a good time. Ronnie looks at him and he glances at her but she turns away. Brother starts on the first page. Ronnie slips out the side exit of the front desk, her shoes squeak quickly down the hall.

RONNIE

Security, security!

Brother stands up and tip toes to the door and again pushes the wrong door. There is the sound of several footsteps galloping his way. He then chooses the right door and quickly walks back to his car, and spins out of the parking lot.

I/E. SIBLING COMMUNITY CENTER- AFTERNOON

Brother is in a sparse parking lot. The community center is a red brick building with many signs and posters on community rights, HIV awareness, voting and funding for the community.

INT. SIBLING COMMUNITY CENTER-MOMENTS LATER

He enters and phones are ringing while several people are passing him in the hall. A couple offices are full of seniors who are speaking inaudibly loud.

Brother enters the community room. MM-HMM is shuffling papers and barking out orders and answering the phone and e-mails. Mm hmm is still on the phone and she motions Brother to sit in a chair in front of her. Throughout the story Mm-hmm talks like a preacher as well as moves like a preacher. She is a community activist.

MM-HMM
My first cousin comes to the seedy part of town?

Brother playfully smiles while simultaneously hitting his alarm on his truck as the horn sounds. She motions for him to sit in front of her.

BROTHER
I was just in the area.

(OS) someone calls her name and refers her to the phone she takes it and speaks, it is inaudible.

MM-HMM
How is it you have time to make a social call?

Brother sits straight up.

BROTHER
You ever remember a Walter Gillespie? A family member.

Mm-hmm still multitasking on her desk.

MM-HMM
There was another brother who just walked away. My daddy use to call him Enoch because he just walked away with God. I don't know if he did but that's the way they saw it.

Brother sits on the edge of his chair looks around then whispers to Mm-hmm, who only knows one loud volume.

BROTHER
I got a call from Belair telling me to pick him up by the weekend.

Mm-hmm freezes almost speechless, recovers and laughs out loud.

MM-HMM
You are lying. Just like that. Where are you going put him? What did Miss Thing say?

Mm-hmm beckons Brother to follow her from desk to desk placing handouts to her staff and signing papers. She looks at the wall where five people are lined up to see her. Someone hands her a clipboard and she points at the first person in line and beckons her to follow Brother.

BROTHER

Are you talking
about Maria?

Mm-hmm cell phone rings, she answers inaudible, and keeps it in her hand while still talking to Brother.

MM-HMM
I know your wife's
name. She a
sweetheart. You
know who I'm
talking about?

Brother shakes his head in disgust.

BROTHER
You two haven't
worked that out
yet. Look I was
hoping we could all
talk about this.
He's family.

Mm-hmm stops and motions that the person waiting to see her to sit. She places her arm around brother and starts walking him toward the door. Mm-hmm's cell phone has someone who is continuing talking.

MM-HMM
Right now we're
busy with the local
elections. I'm not
sure our schedules
makes anything do-
able.

BROTHER
We can't take him
in, somebody else
could, or should.

Mm-hmm looks him straight in the eye, straightening his garments, speaks to the cell phone, hangs up and then speaks to brother.

MM-HMM

I'll call you back mayor! Brother the phone call was to you and your house. I raised my children and I'm not raising any man. A man needs to keep up with me. I'll help out whatever way I can but from this office only.

BROTHER

I have the same situation. I can't take him, even if he's the only senior besides you.

She shoots a sharp look at him for questioning her age.

MM-HMM

Watch it Brother! I got some seniors in my office who will take you if I tell them to. Bye! Call me when we meet.

I/E. SIBILING COMMUNITY CENTER PARKING LOT MOMENTS-LATER

Brother is entering car and shouts back at Mm-hmm

BROTHER

Are you going to call Miss Thing or me?

He pulls away laughing at her and she shouts back within earshot.

MM-HMM

I ain't calling her
for nothing!

I/E. COMESEE'S HOME-DAY

Brother is standing outside his sister COMESEE's apartment. He is sitting and removing his work boots. He straightening his white athletic socks, takes a quick whiff of his feet and his eyes flutter as he wipes his nose. DEUCE, Brother's dingy wife-beater one-arm cousin opens the door. Brother forces a smile but it's unreal. They lightly bump forearms as he enters the house.

The apartment is filled with tan thick foam in place of major furniture. It also has places cut out where real furniture sits. It's like continuingly walking on giant foam from couch cushions.

BROTHER
Where's Comesee?

DEUCE
She's in the back.
She knows you're
here! Sit down
cousin.
Deuce wipes his
nose and looks at
Brother's feet.
Brother sharply
looks at Deuce.

BROTHER
I know what to do
in my sister house.

Brother sits as Deuce folds his blankets and picks up his top shirt and pants from the foam couch.

Brother shakes his head and looks for his sister in the back.

DEUCE
Are you still in business and in plumbing school?

Brother looks at him and stares.

BROTHER
Yeah I still have a job. You still using?

Brother nods at the fresh needle tracks on Deuce's arm. Deuce, rubs his arm. Brother shouts for Comesee.

DEUCE
That's your first shot.

BROTHER
Comesee, I don't have all day!

Brother awkwardly stands up on the foam, looking for his sister.

DEUCE
I'm working for Comesee this week.

Brother for the first time looks around the house, which is clean.

BROTHER
You still can clean a house.

Deuce smiles and grabs a dust cloth wiping the foam and clearing the dishes he left from the last night.

BROTHER
How long you staying?

Brother is interrupted by his sister COMESEE.

COMESEE

Deuce knows how long he can stay and when he has to go. Why you here brother of mine?

She sits as Deuce offers a couple of glasses of red Kool-Aid full of white sugar at the bottom. He places the glasses besides Comesee and Brother in a cutout section of the chair and couch. They tilt.

COMESEE
You forgot the coasters Deuce.

Deuce snaps his fingers, leaves and returns with the coasters. Brother surveys the sugar in the glass and slowly puts it down. Deuce scratches, eyeing the glass. Brother looks at Deuce as if he shouldn't be here but continues anyway.

BROTHER
We got this problem.

He looks around.

BROTHER
Where the kids?

Comesee takes a big swig of the Kool-Aid as Brother winces and Deuce points to Brother's glass and he motions for him not to take it and Deuce takes it anyway. Deuce gulps down a fourth and returns it.

COMESEE
This ain't a social visit. Let me enjoy this quiet! What's up?

DEUCE
Yeah what's up?

Brother rolls his eyes at Deuce but continues.

BROTHER
I saw Mm-hmm and she told me about.

Deuce interrupts Brother.

DEUCE
She's suppose to let me clean her house next week!

BROTHER
Did you say clean her out or sleep on her couch?

DEUCE
That's two and three man, don't let this one arm fool you. I'll go street on you!

Deuce smiles sinisterly but Brother waves it off. Comesee shouts at Brother. Brother stands

COMESEE
Brother! Tell the story.

Brother lumbers around the room telling them about the Uncle Walter and Mm-hmm's encounter.

COMESEE
What does this have to do with me?

BROTHER
We as a family have to make a decision on whose going to keep Uncle Walter.

Comesee takes another Kool-Aide swig, and has difficulty getting up out of the foam chair, while Deuce grabs at her with his one arm and she nearly breaks his only arm.

COMESEE
I got kids and a husband. We can't raise nobody else's child. With the older you have to watch them, feed them, and medicines. All that stuff you do for babies. I can't go backwards. You're the family they called!

She walks in the dining area motioning for Brother to follow her. He does followed by Deuce. She stands at the break-front and looks at the nice china and reaches inside pulls out paper plates and hands them to Brother. She points for him to walk in opposite directions.

COMESEE
Where's he been? Is he really a Gillespie? Did you talk to him? What he say?

Brother places the paper plates around the table as Comesee places forks and cups walking in opposite direction. She looks at Deuce who has somehow gone and got the Kool-Aid and returned without missing a second of conversation and is waiting for her orders to pour.

BROTHER
I don't know to all those questions.

Comesee nods toward Deuce. Deuce pours the Kool-Aid. He struggles with one arm, pouring each cup with precision, and proportion.

COMESEE
Who else did you talk to?

DEUCE
Did you talk to my sister?

Brother and Comesee look at each and then away from each other.

BROTHER
I was hoping you'd call her or have seen her.

COMESEE
I haven't seen her. I talked to her a couple weeks ago.

Brother surveys the table.

BROTHER
I don't smell anything cooking.

COMESEE
If you hungry you go home. The way you ate when we was kids, we don't want to adopt you. Second, it smells better than those feet you hauling around.

Deuce and Comesee crack-up and Brother is embarrassed. He starts for the door.

DEUCE
I'll take him.

Brother walks back in dining room and grabs the napkins from a draw and places them around the table.

COMESEE
Deuce, how can you take care of a senior citizen, you barely making it.

BROTHER
I'm surprise we having this conversation with a dope fein.

DEUCE
You blowing my high man. Don't be here when I come down.

Deuce starts scratching a little more and has to put the Kool-Aide pitcher down.

COMESEE
Calm down Deuce and finish what you were saying.

DEUCE
I use to be junkie and a dope fein, but now I'm a addict. There are a lot of addicts out there. Which one are you?

COMESEE
Deuce you don't need to explain.

She is interrupted by Brother touching her arm.

BROTHER
No, Comesee let this fool keep going. I have to hear this.

Deuce motions for them to have a seat. Comesee stands and Brother sits with a sarcastic smile.

DEUCE

He should stay with me. He homeless, I'm homeless. All our family members has couches. Uncle Walter's old, maybe he's going die in a little and everybody wants family close when they about to die. I am only one who was close to death when I fell off the roof.

In unison, Comesee and Brother shout out.

BROTHER/COMESEE

You were pushed!

Deuce rubs his shoulder of his missing arm.

DEUCE

That arm save me, it just couldn't save itself. That's the story I'm sticking to

Brother's mouth is wide open. He checks his watch and heads for the door. Comesee follows him as Deuce holds up his one arm looking for a response. He turns and heads back to living room. Brother and Comesee are at her front door. There are sounds of school buses and children in a distance.

BROTHER

You know he's right about one thing, he addicted to a lot of.

COMESEE
Brother, don't curse in my house!

BROTHER
OK, you know he better not stay longer than . . .

Comesee interrupts him.

COMESEE
Two days. I know. I just need him to clean a little more.

BROTHER
We don't call him, Deuce for nothing.

In unison beyond earshot, they chuckle as they speak.

BROTHER/COMESEE
More than two days space, Deuce will case and hit your place!

Brother and Comesee embrace as he opens the door a row of stair step children enter and hug their Uncle.

I/E. COMESEE'S HOME-LATE AFTERNOON

Brother is sitting on the stairs putting his shoes back on amongst the kids taking theirs off. He teases them and vice versa. He looks at Comesee.

BROTHER
Talk to his sister. I'll contact the out-of-towners.

She gives him a thumbs up sign, while counting her kids and looking up and down the street for stragglers.

BROTHER
You never told me what's for dinner.

COMESEE
Its called what-you-get is what-we-got

They both laugh and mouth I-love-you- to each other and Brother gets in his truck and Comesee closes her gates.

INT. JUDGE'S APARTMENT-DAY

JUDGE is a high profile corporate attorney and multitasking morning activities. Judge's apartment is scattered with clothing, cell, and paperwork for the morning race to work.

INT. ELEVATOR LOBBY-MOMENTS LATER

She snatches her keys, locks the door and darts for the elevator. She decides to take the stairs. Judge opens the stairwell door, and is startled by Deuce. She jumps into a martial arts position and yells.

JUDGE
On guard!

Deuce stops, and laughs.

DEUCE
Girl, what are you studying now? Don't you recognize your own brother?

Judge slowly comes out of her stance and stares at Deuce, not immediately recognizing him, looks closer.

JUDGE

Deuce?

Deuce raises his one hand up and Judge relaxes.

JUDGE
I didn't have my contacts in. What are you doing here? Walk me down.

Judge stops and looks up behind her and Deuce hasn't moved. He has a crooked smile and his one thumb pointing back toward the apartment.

JUDGE
Don't even- no! It's not my couch's turn, I haven't seen you in two months or talked to you. I'm on my way to work. Come on.

They descend the stairwell quick and exit the building.

EXT. SIDEWALK-DAY MOMENTS LATER

Judge and Deuce walk toward the train station, with people walking in all directions.

DEUCE
I'm thinking about getting a roommate.

Judge looks at him and almost spills her cappuccino on her suit.

JUDGE
Go on.

Deuce tells Judge about Uncle Walter and his plan. They descend the train's steps.

INT. TRAIN STATION MOMENTS-LATER

Judge digs in her purse and gets a subway token, when she looks up Deuce is gone. She looks around for him and there's no sight of him. She drops her token in the turn-stile and enters the platform. She turns to the left and Deuce is there.

DEUCE

So what do you think?

JUDGE

How? What? I'm an officer of the court I could get in trouble because you jumped the turn-stile.

DEUCE

Didn't jump, that's for two handed people. The one-handers have to.

Judge raises her hand and shakes her head negatively.

JUDGE

I don't want to know, how long are you planning on riding with me?

DEUCE

Are you swearing me in?

Judge is embarrassed her hand is still up, she lowers it, as a train rumbles pass.

JUDGE

I don't have free time because I'm single. I can't care for a pet, how am I suppose to

minister to an
Uncle no one knows.

DEUCE
Do you think I can
do it?

JUDGE
My trains coming,
you're not getting
on with me dressed
like that.

DEUCE
Maybe, I need to
show up and watch
my sister work.

She shows the hand again.

DEUCE
Are you swearing me
in again?

She snatches her hand down.

JUDGE
I have some career
goals.

DEUCE
That's what Mm-hmm
said about you.

JUDGE
What and when did
she say that?

The train settles in for a stop and the doors open and people pour in and out. Judge and Deuce enter.

JUDGE
OK OK. Tell
everybody to meet
at my place on
Saturday after my
yoga conference.

Deuce inserts his one hand in the closing door and pushes it open. He squeezes himself through people who move out of his way because of his dingy wife beater tee shirt. He exits and shouts to Judge.

DEUCE

They opened up like the red sea.

He pumps his one arm. Judge waves at her brother from inside the train-car. He never looked back, instead picks something off the ground and swallows it.

JUDGE

How did that fool get into my apartment building?

Dejected, Judge softly and continuously bumps her forehead against the plastic window as the train rumbles away.

INT. JUDGE'S APARTMENT-THREE DAYS LATER

Judge runs to the door because of the feverish knocking. Judge glances through the peephole then falls back against the door and closes her eyes and softly bangs the back of her head on the door. She opens it and her entire family enters pushing her behind the door.

COMESEE

I know you heard us knocking.
Everybody's coming.

Comesee walks around exploring the place.

Brother comes in with his children as well as Comesee's kids.

BROTHER

Judge, I'm glad you volunteered your place, that's the kind of family attitude all of us need.

JUDGE
Where's Deuce?

COMESEE
Mm-hmm is bringing him. While we're here, my girls have to get their hair done.

BROTHER
Deuce said you were having a just because party, and you needed family.

JUDGE
A just because party. I don't remember saying anything about a party.

BROTHER
Just because we're here for something else, don't mean we shouldn't have a party. Family is still coming.

Other family members are making themselves at home, cooking their own food, and doing hair. Judge is constantly going from room to room chiding them, and when she leaves they continue what they were doing.

JUDGE
Why are all of you here so late?

COMESEE
Deuce said you had to do something with yogurt, we

figured you'd be finish by now.

JUDGE

I finished the yoga conference early this morning.

BROTHER

If you had a conference, it sure doesn't look like many people showed up.

JUDGE

It was an online conference.

Brother, Comesee and other family members laugh and look at each other

BROTHER/COMESEE

OK, right.

COMESEE

Girl, you had a conference with people, that wasn't here but was some place else, and you talked about yogurt? How'd they know you were eating it?

BROTHER

That's not a conference that's breakfast conversation. You wasn't on line, you was lying down.

Everyone laughs again. Judge chuckles, but keeps her composure as the doorbell rings. She walks over to open it and shouts back.

JUDGE
It's not yogurt its yoga.

Judge face drops when she sees Deuce and Mm-hmm. She nods to them both and walks away leaving them to close the door.

MM-HMM
I'm coming to your house and you not going to speak?

Judge turns around.

JUDGE
I nodded, why you want a special greeting. You should speak first since this is your first and last time here.

Deuce jumps in the middle of them and attempts to hold off one with his hand and the other with his shoulder which throws him off balance. Other family members hear the loud voices and walk over.

DEUCE
Judge, this is Mm-hmm first time being here.

Everyone looks at him, and he just throws up his one arm as if asking what did he say, that caused the stare.

BROTHER
We don't have all day. Everybody bring their food and do all the hair in the living room.

The entire family gathers around the couch. Brother snatches the remote from one of the older teens and shuts off the computer game. There are eight adults present.

BROTHER

I talked with the four family members out- of- town. Whatever we agree on about Uncle Walter is OK. Is there anyone who want's to take Uncle Walter in, signal by a raising two hands.

Brother gives a look at Deuce and smiles, No one else budges.

DEUCE

You are blowing my high man. I don't want to be you when I come back down.

Brother poses with both his biceps showing, mocking Deuce. Deuce raises up and walks in one direction but darts toward Brother. MM-hmm jumps between them and tries to maintain order. Brother edges him on.

BROTHER

Come on you leech, you shouldn't be in any of this conversation or here.

DEUCE

Let him go, I'll leech on him. Who put you in-charge? You're not the leader of this family. Why does everyone have to listen to you? You ain't nobody. You've been in school too long anyway. You should be taking care of your kids and sweet Maria.

Brother lunges at him, but family is holding him back while other family are near Deuce, but he standing still, with his hand behind his back. Maria walks up behind Brother and lightly touches his shoulders.

MARIA

Brother?

Brother immediately calms down. He takes Maria's hand and he sits on the couch and the kids assemble beside him. He drops his head ashamed. Deuce sits down, still eyeing Brother. Deuce pulls his hand out of his pocket and a needled syringe falls to the floor. He kicks it under a couch before anyone recognizes it. Mm-hmm stands.

MM-HMM

We trust your decision Brother. You're doing the right thing.

There is an echo from the family, encouraging him on. Brother stands and hands out calendars to the adults. Brother drops the additional four calendars on the coffee table.

BROTHER

Since there's twelve of us, each of us are going to have to take him for one month out of the year, I've assigned the months.

There are loud shouts, people are screaming about their months. Finally, Judge calms them down by bringing in some brunch smoothies she created.

MM-HMM

Nobody else volunteered to help? It's a better idea than I would have thought of, but I just can't work this thing in May.

The crowd noise and debate starts up again.

JUDGE

We need to calm down in here. This isn't a tenement, this is a condo.

MM-HMM

Use to be, before you and your corporations moved uptown.

JUDGE

Whatever, you're just bitter Mm-hmm.

Mm-hmm looks at Judge unnerving.

MM-HMM

Excuse me Miss, I mean Ms. Thing what do I have to be bitter about?

Judge walks toward another room, visually picking and replacing items that were out place.

JUDGE

Believe me, you don't want to go there.

Comesee is braiding her daughter's hair, and watching her cousins like a tennis match.

COMESEE
Why every time we come together you two always have an argument?

JUDGE
She's jealous of me.

Mm-hmm puts her hands on her hips and snaps her fingers twice and waves her away.

MM-HMM
Your job has you power tripping.

There is a severe knock at the door. Judge puts her finger over her mouth for everyone's silence. She tip- toes to the peephole. Mm-hmm charges at Judge because of the gesture, but sits down at the knock again. Judge whispers after not recognizing the face outside the door.

JUDGE
I told you, this is a condo and we have a noise ordinance. Maybe they'll stop if we be quiet.

COMESEE
Judge, did you pay your rent. It could be the landlord.

JUDGE
Excuse me. I have a mortgage.

MM-HMM
See her arrogance.

Mm-hmm motions for the others to notice her apartment's opulence.

Deuce charges toward the door and opens it amongst family members motioning him to stop. In walks an old man carrying a brief case. The family is stunned at the gentleman. Deuce ushers him in and takes his bag, as Brother takes the bag from Deuce.

COMESEE
Hi, how are you doing?

Everyone echo's the question.

OLD MAN
Hello everyone.

BROTHER
Hey, Ah who. . .

Brother is pushed away, everyone embraces him, Brother is reluctant.

OLD MAN
Thank you all very much. I wasn't expecting this. It has been a long day.

MM-HMM
We know it has been quite a while. Where have you been?

OLD MAN
I've traveling throughout.

Judge interrupts.

JUDGE
Are you hungry? Get Uncle something to eat. I made some smoothies, someone else is cooking

and someone is braiding hair. Just a normal day at my condo.

She blushes and emphasize that's it's her condo. Everyone ignores her.

MM-HMM

Let Uncle talk instead of trying to feed him . . .

The old man interrupts.

OLD MAN

I thank you for such a title especially since we just met.

COMESEE

We respect our elders, and you're the oldest in the room.

He's not sure how to respond to the compliment or curse. He is a little embarrassed.

OLD MAN

Thank you, there is something I'd.

Deuce walks around him, scratching himself and shakes hands with the old man.

The old man is a little uncomfortable, with Deuce walking completely around him, and looking at him up and down.

DEUCE

How come you walk so slow? Is it because you're old?

A family member pulls Deuce away from the old man, because he's a close talker. He allows them to pull him away.

DEUCE
Everyone wants to know.

The old man chuckles and takes a sip of the smoothie and a bite of the chicken and motions everything is great. He removes a chicken and hair from his mouth. No one reacts because they are eating also and talking amongst themselves and the old man.

OLD MAN
I'll answer his question, I just have old bunions.

The family looks at each other and cracks up.

BROTHER
Sir, we're glad you can laugh but I have some questions.

OLD MAN
Thank you. I've always enjoyed laughter, even at work we.

MM-HMM
You work? Where?

OLD MAN
I did, but I'm retired and I hang around at the. . .

Comesee interrupts.

COMESEE
At the nursing home? I thought you live there.

DEUCE
Now he can live with us.

Everyone motions for Deuce to settle down and be quiet. Deuce is dejected and exits the room. All eyes are on the old man.

OLD MAN
No, I go to the Hall, and there's something I'd like to show you, if I can have my bag back.

Mm-hmm squeezes her way through the crowd of questions.

MMHMM
I heard you say hall. You a union man? Are you from the union hall of longshoremen?

INT. JUDGE'S APARTMENT-BATHROOM MINUTES LATER

Deuce locks the door. He reaches in his back pocket for the syringe. He removes the commode's lid and removes a plastic bag. He takes out a bent spoon, lighter and a long rubber band. He takes off one shoe and dirty sock. In another pocket he pulls out heroin pack and pours it in the spoon. He drips some saliva on the spoon. He puts the handle in his mouth, lights bottom of the spoon.

Someone knocks. He stamps his other foot twice and the knocking ceases. Deuce licks his lips. He steps on rubber band with his bare-feet and wraps the band between his toes and foot and his veins enlarge. Deuce then takes the cap off the syringe with his mouth, spits it the floor, and he smiles. He inserts the needle into liquid and draws back. He injects his instep. He leaves the needle in and sits back on the commode.

JUDGE'S APARTMENT-MOMENTS LATER

The old man smiles and pulls out his wallet fumbling with other business cards. He can't find one.

OLD MAN
No, no, I'm not a longshoreman.

BROTHER
How did you find us?

OLD MAN
I drove here.

COMESEE
You have a car? Were you in the Army?

The old man looks at her directly.

OLD MAN
No, we don't believe in the military.

Brother stands and begins pacing around him.

BROTHER
All our dads served this country. I thought all guys your age did the pledge, the armed force thing!

Old man stops Brother in his pacing and places a hand on his shoulder. Brother quickly looks at his hand on his shoulder and the old man quickly removes it. Brother continues moving.

MARIA

Don't matter him Uncle, we'd just like to know a little about you. I guess you must have had good federal job.

OLD MAN

We just don't believe in government jobs, nor the any kind of pledge.

COMESEE

Not even the pledge of allegiance

The old man shakes his head and everyone stares at him. Tia takes the glass out of the old man's hand while he sipping on it. The family ignores it.

BROTHER

Are you still American? Everybody salutes the flag even Deuce. Where is he?

Everyone searches the room, no Deuce.

MM-HMM

Deuce! Deuce!

One of the younger children who's twisting and turning points to the bathroom door.

MARIA

He's been in there a while.

BROTHER

Excuse me sir.

INT. JUDGE'S APARTMENT HALL-OUTSIDE BATHROOM DOOR

Brother leaves the living room and knocks. The bathroom door opens quick and Deuce exits, as the nephew shoots in and slams the door. Deuce and Brother eye each other up and down. Deuce walks back to living room. Brother follows.

INT. JUDGE'S APARTMENT LIVING ROOM MOMENTS LATER.

Deuce sits on the couch and Brother stands visually searching the old man.

COMESEE
With all do respect
for your age sir
are you one of
those commuters
from Russia or Red
China.

Judge drops her head in disgust, at Comesee's inappropriate word. Mm-hmm see this and responds.

MM-HMM
At least she's not
afraid to pursue
the truth.

Judge turns her head in the direction of Old man. Her back is facing Mm-hmm, who becomes furious and packs her belonging. Comesee grabs her shoulder and starts braiding her hair. Mm-hmm relaxes.

JUDGE
We were just about
to find out where
was the best place
for you.

The old man stands, looking for his briefcase.

OLD MAN
If I could, please have my brief case, I'd like to show you all something.

Old man looks at Deuce on the couch in a deep nod. He is sitting but is leaned over with his chest resting on his thighs.

OLD MAN
What's he do? Work nights?

No one answers. Someone tilts Deuce back and he soon duplicates the nod.

COMESEE
He's does shift work in urban pharmacy.

The family lightly chuckles and shameful smiles. Old man doesn't get it.

MM-HMM
Is that the only bag you have? Give him his bag. I hope you didn't bring anything for us.

One of Comesee's children hands the old man his brief case. He holds up his hand and the family is captivated. He reaches into his bag and pulls out a watchtower booklet and Jehovah Witness Bible.

OLD MAN
I'm with the Jehovah Witnesses and we like you to know the truth about the bible.

The family's mouths are open and they all stand simultaneously. Maria quickly steps in between them and the old man. He is still clueless.

MARIA
If I may, on behalf of the immediate family I have one question. Are you or have ever been Walter Gillespie?

OLD MAN
No, my name is Jesse Wilford, but my friends call me JW. Its ironic JW, and Jehovah Witness. I think that's pretty catchy.

The old man chuckles at his own joke but no one else is smiling. Maria quickly gets out of the middle of the floor. In unison everyone points toward the door. Their arms are motioning go, go, go. The old man is not moving faster enough and the entire family moves in toward him and there is a rumble.

EXT. JUDGE'S APARTMENT-HALLWAY MOMENTS LATER

The old man's clothing is disheveled and he's sitting on the floor. The apartment door opens and his brief case is hurled out toward him, he catches it and walks down the hall.

OLD MAN
Haters.

INT.FUNERAL HOME OFFICE.DAY

Dern and Fern are still cleaning the vaulted room. They are picking through trash boxes.

They open one box and it has a suitcase full of male clothing.

DERN
What are we going to do with these suits?

FERN
Why don't you keep them? They look like they could fit you.

DERN
Do you think Billy, I mean Bill-lee would let me have them?

FERN
He's not standing right here bucket head, you can call him Billy.

Dern surveys the dim lit office.

DERN
How we know they aren't looking at us from one of those open circus cameras?

FERN
Because on the outside of the building, the sign says the bank ruptured a pipe or something. That's why they closing, and we working.

DERN
There's not any pair of long johns

in the bunch. If you wouldn't have sneezed we could have sent it to everybody.

Fern shrugs her shoulders

FERN

Send it to the Gil-les-pie guy's people. There was a shovel full of them.

Dern is fumbling through more clothing. It is different suits, ties and shirts but nothing matches and he makes a discovery.

DERN

There's some lady clothes in here. You want them? They are Sunday school clothes.

Fern walks over and starts looking through them.

FERN

They aren't my size, besides I'm waiting for the clearance rack at Cracker Barrel.

Dern boxes the materials, and Fern helps. They stuff the clothing in different sizes boxes and suitcases. It looks very uncoordinated and sloppy.

DERN

You don't think the family, will hate the clothes we're sending?

They both stand up and look at the boxes and suitcase.

FERN
You're right Dern, we need to fold the stuff.

They take the men and women clothing out of the boxes and fold neatly and precisely which fit in the boxes and suitcase.

INT. BROTHER'S HOME/DAY TWO DAYS LATER

Brother, Maria, and Tia are having breakfast along with the other two children.

BROTHER
OK baby, have I done everything you needed me to do?

Maria nods her head yes, and shakes her head at the uniqueness of her husband.

BROTHER
Kids, for the next five minutes I need to be left alone. Keep eating but don't asking me anything.

Brother pours his dry cereal and picks up the milk. Brother gives a thumbs up sign. His family gives the thumbs up sign. Brother pours his milk, grabs the spoon and rapidly eats. Brother's mouth is full and he leans back in his chair then forward for three more thick scoops. The doorbell rings. His head drops and Maria motions she'll get it but he touches her hand. He grabs his spoon, bowl and eats walking to the door. He opens it.

I/E. BROTHER'S HOME/DAY DOOR OPEN- MOMENTS LATER

Brother drops his spoon and food remains in his mouth. In his doorway is an older man with suitcases. Maria appears and catches the bowl from falling to the floor and picks up the spoon.

MARIA
Can I help you sir?

DELIVERY MAN
Yes, is this the Gillespie residence?

MARIA
Yes, it is.

He puts the bags down. Brother stutters.

BROTHER
Your name is not Walter is it?

DELIVERY MAN
As a matter of fact, this stuff came from a guy named Walter.

MARIA
Just the two suitcases?

DELIVERY MAN
Nope, there's a couple or three more boxes and another suitcase. Where do you want to put them?

BROTHER
Just follow me.

INT. BROTHER'S HOME-DINING ROOM-MOMENTS LATER

Dejected Brother leads the delivery man into the dining room. He gets the bowl and spoon from Maria, sits back at the table, stares into his bowl, and lightly stirring his cereal.

TIA
Daddy, aren't you going to finish your cereal? That's what you tell the twins.

He looks at her sarcastically, while she laughs, madly texting.

BROTHER
Its soup now, don't you have more people to text?

The delivery man drops the suitcase and exits. He returns with several more boxes and another suitcase. He holds out his signature book and Brother signs it. Maria enters the room.

DELIVERY MAN
I hate soggy flakes too.

Brother points twice toward the door. Delivery man laughs but won't leave.

DELIVERY MAN
I guess you won't be needing this receipt although it's sort of crunchy.

Brother again points toward the exit. He does so. Maria motions the children to exit and Maria follows them.

MARIA
Call me if you need me.

BROTHER

Maria, Maria,
Maria!

MARIA
I didn't mean that soon. I wasn't serious. He's your Uncle you need to check his stuff.

BROTHER
Yeah, but this is our house and his stuff is in our house.

MARIA
It's only suppose to be for a month, remember.

Brother nods his head he and Maria opens boxes separately. Each item they show the other. They both pull out panties and bras from different boxes.

BROTHER
You don't think?

MARIA
I don't know what to think? I knew I didn't want to help you. There are dresses in here too.

BROTHER
I can't think. I don't know if anybody was into that back then.

MARIA
You mean being gay? That's always been around.

BROTHER

No, wearing women's clothes.

MARIA
Your family has some surprises.

BROTHER
Yeah, I mean no. Its hard enough to get the family to keep him for a month, but nobody's expecting him to switch panties and boxers, and vice versa.

MARIA
How do we know there his? There are different sizes of men suits and dresses.

BROTHER
None of us are the same size we were a week ago. Maybe he had a weight problem.

Maria continues going through the materials and separating the items.

MARIA
What size is he?

BROTHER
I don't know. I was a kid when he was a man or a. . . Why does it matter? I'm throwing stuff away anyway.

MARIA
No you're not.

BROTHER
What are you
talking about?

Maria stops separating the clothing and walks out of the room. She returns moments later with several hangers. She gives them to Brother.

MARIA
Hang them up. All
of them. These are
his clothes.

Brother refuses to move. He watches Maria. He puts the hangers on top of the clothes.

BROTHER
How can we keep
this stuff that may
not be his?

Maria grabs some of the suits and assembles them and also hangs them up.

MARIA
Its not up to us.
Uncle Walter will
let go of what he
doesn't want.

Brother looks at the volume of material and throws up his hands.

BROTHER
Where are we
suppose to keep it?

MARIA
The attic or the
basement. There's
plenty of room.

BROTHER
No way! Out of
sight out of mind.
You know if it gets
put away, it will
stay.

Maria grabs more clothes from Brother's stack. Brother hands her more of his.

MARIA
We could put it all in your closet, so you will see it everyday.

BROTHER
That's funny, real funny. This is women stuff, he's a man, why would he want to keep this stuff? I'm going to ask him this weekend.

Maria puts the clothing down and points a hanger at Brother threatening him.

MARIA
Don't do that. You're just meeting him for the first time.

BROTHER
A man needs to know these things. I need to know before he comes into my house around my children and wife.

MARIA
You sound so prejudiced.

Brother throws the clothes up in the air and then lays on top of them.

BROTHER
That's the last thing I thought you ever call me. I'm

concerned about my
family.

MARIA

You're more
concerned about
your self. You're
so macho, just like
my brothers.

Brother looks up from the floor at Maria. He sits up with his head in his hands.

BROTHER

Why did you say
something like
that?

MARIA

How would you feel
if somebody who you
had not seen in
ages walked up to
you and asked you
whether you wore
men or women
clothes or both?

BROTHER

I wasn't going to
ask him that quick.
I was going to get
to it before we got
home.

Brother stands and grabs his share of the clothing back and hangs them. Maria hands him some women clothing and he looks around as if someone is seeing him and hangs them quick.

MARIA

If you decide to
have that
conversation with
Uncle Walter, it
may back fire on
you.

Brother laughs.

BROTHER
How's that?

MARIA
Uncle Walter may check you out, or wonder about you.

Brother slams his hands against his legs.

BROTHER
What is a man suppose to do?

MARIA
Be a nephew and welcome him home.

INT. SHOPPING CENTER-DAY

Mm-hmm and Comesee walk the mall. Comesee's children are circling them and running up ahead.

MM-HMM
What do you think we should do?

COMESEE
Don't know, I've haven't told Basil yet.

Mm-hmm stops at a palette of toilet paper and motions to the kids. The kids scrabble and toss a dozen rolls and jet onward.

MM-HMM
That's asking a lot for people to change their routine. I refuse to take care of any man.

COMESEE

He's family, but he ain't family. Nobody's seen or met him.

MM-HMM

So what, he's our daddy's brother. The man disappeared. I just can't change my life because he showed up.

Comesee looks at some children's socks, underwear and small items. Mm-hmm nods. She places items in her cart. They both go to women's clearance. Comesee holds up skirt to her waist.

COMESEE

How you like me now?

Mm-hmm smiles and waves at her.

MM-HMM

You know I use to be that size.

Comesee puts the dress down, Mm-hmm frowns.

COMESEE

We just don't know the man. You know Basil, he's a spiritual man, he doesn't allow anyone he doesn't know in our home.

One of the kids walk over.

SMALL CHILD

Sister told me to ask you can we have hamburgers at McDonald.

COMESEE
Sure, you can have some hamburgers at Mc-home.

The kid darts away elated, then abruptly stops.

Mmm-hmm and Comesee both laugh, the kid doesn't think its funny.

MM-HMM
Raise them girl!

COMESEE
They know better.

MM-HMM
How are we going to help Brother? I just have too much to do in the community, to just deal with one person.

Tia walks up and speaks to her aunts and walks with the ladies. She's looking at clothing, boys and still texting. Mm-hmm and Comesee, shrug their shoulders. Tia bumps into several people because she's texting and walking.

COMESEE
Little girl, you better watch where you going. I don't want to fight in any mall.

Mm-hmm grabs at the phone but, Tia respectfully pulls away.

MM-HMM
What are you texting that you can't watch where you going?

Tia stops texting for thirty seconds.

TIA
Nothing auntie,
just some friends.

The two aunts look at her with admiration and trust. They arrive at the fruit and nut counter as the other kids circle around them waiting instructions. They try to see Tia's text but she refuses to show them.

MM-HMM
This is the first time I've seen your face without your head down in that phone. You're a beautiful little girl.

TIA
Yes ma'am.

COMESEE
You remember she said little. You're little at 13.

TIA
I'm 14, auntie.

COMESEE
Don't matter much. You're still a little girl.

MM-HMM
That means put the phone down and help.

Reluctantly, Tia closes her phone and starts gathering fruits and veggies. The kids are examining the fruits trying to pick out the best bananas, apples etc.

COMESEE

I think everybody feels the same way about the fruitcake coming.

MM-HMM

You right. I don't think none of our family likes fruitcake. We'll hold it for a month. . . .

COMESEE

Then pass it on to other family.

They both nod their heads in agreement. Their shopping cart is almost full. They pile fruits and vegetables inside the cart.

COMESEE

You always buy for the center?

MM-HMM

I'm accountable for the grant. I want to make sure what's in the account is counted out right.

COMESEE

You got that right. You never know what's in a fruitcake.

Tia reacts to a text by laughing. Her Aunts look at her, she glances at them and she puts the phone in her pocket.

MM-HMM

You got that right. Unless you baked it, you don't know what's in it.

COMESEE
Or where it's been,
or where its going.
Everybody can't
cook in our family.

Mm-hmm looks at her and pauses, examining a grapefruit.

MM-HMM
I know you're not
talking about me.

COMESEE
No, but that is one
way to get and keep
a man.

Mm-hmm drops the grapefruit in the basket and continues on, followed by Comesee and the kids.

MM-HMM
This kitchen is
closed. It's been
open enough.

COMESEE
You're right, a
closed refrigerator
stays cold.

MM-HMM
I had too many
people putting what
they want in there;
salad, cold cuts,
hot food, beer,
wine, and
everything.

COMESEE
That's what a
fridge is for, what
do you expect?

MM-HMM
I was the only one
not putting

something in. They took what I had in the beginning, middle and end. When I looked inside, it was full of stuff and it stank.

There is a pause as the kids bring fruit and nuts to the cart. Mm-hmm and Comesee continue shopping.

COMESEE
We're suppose to be helping Brother, not ourselves.

MM-HMM
I am helping Brother. How you figure I'm helping myself?

COMESEE
No fruitcake.

MM-HMM
Just because my fridge is finally clean, I'm going to put what I want in it. I can't let nobody else put what they want inside.

COMESEE
You’re suppose to be a community activist and help people.

MM-HMM
I help the community outside my home, not inside. Plus,

fruitcake ain't community, he's one.

COMESEE

Are you just going to leave fruitcake?

MM-HMM

Let it become a door holder, or pass it on. Just not my door.

COMESEE

You never liked fruitcakes did you?

The family enters the area where there are toys and Tia grabs another buggy. Comesee shakes her head no, but Mm-hmm taps her chest. They become more excited, pulling on their auntie to go to all the aisles at the same time. Comesee follows behind with her overflowing cart.

MM-HMM

I'm learning to like what I bake. I don't hear you offering no ideas about helping Brother.

COMESEE

We have too many kids!

MM-HMM

What other excuse you have? Nobody told you to lay up with your man and have so many!

COMESEE
Mm-hmm, you better check yourself. You could talk about me all day but my kids and my Basil are off limits.

MM-HMM
Oh, since my kids are up and gone, You could talk about what I'm doing or what I shouldn't! No, you check yourself!

Comesee and Mm-hmm glare at each other hard. They move on down the aisle.

MM-HMM
Did you talk to Miss Thing?

COMESEE
Why you keep calling Judge outside her name? That's why yawl don't talk.

MM-HMM
At least I'll say it to her face. Besides what is she doing to help Brother?

COMESEE
Why you so worried about her? What's up between you two?

MM-HMM
That ain't none of your business.

COMESEE

If I didn't have these kids here and Tia shadowing us like the sun, I'd go off on you telling me to mine my business.

Mm-hmm rolls her eyes.

MM-HMM

Comesee, you can talk all that trash if you want, but Judge and you don't scare me.

COMESEE

Ain't no body trying to scare you, but you too have to come together about Uncle Walter.

MM-HMM

I told you where I stand.

Mm-hmm abruptly turns her shopping cart and goes to the checkout line. Comesee and the kids look at her and enter a line adjacent to her. Comesee puts her stuff on conveyer belt, as does Mm-hmm. They are not looking at each other

COMESEE

She and Deuce are working on something.

This gets Mm-hmm attention.

MM-HMM

Deuce is with her?

COMESEE

That is his sister.

MM-HMM
Those two are never together. Who you think got him in the program? It wasn't her.

COMESEE
I guess that would be you.

Sarcastically, as she looks at Mm-hmm, she slams some cans on the belt angrily.

MM-HMM
How could he do that to me? The organization has done a lot for him.

COMESEE
You helped Deuce. He's one person and you won't help Fruitcake?

MM-HMM
I've known him all my life. We raised each other.

COMESEE
You help him in the community but you can't help another?

MM-HMM
That's just the way it is.

COMESEE
Fruitcake is part of community.

MM-HMM

But for how long? We get a lot of people who come in and use our resources and leave. Then when we need for our local people the well is dry. I don't know this fruitcake.

COMESEE
They say fruitcakes last a long time.

MM-HMM
It depends on if you keep them or pass them on.

COMESEE
Who you mad at?

MM-HMM
You, Miss thing, and Deuce.

COMESEE
What do I have to do with it?

MM-HMM
You knew about Deuce and Miss Thing, and you just telling me. You wrong!

COMESEE
It ain't about you. Why do you think everything is about you?

Both lines are being held up by the two women arguing. The children as well as Tia, are standing in the middle watching the match.

MM-HMM
You've got a lot of issues. You should be helping Brother, and stay out of everybody else's Kool Aide.

COMESEE
Are you flipping on me?

Mm-hmm cuts an eye at Comesee. Then at the kids and then the people behind her. A manager walks up. Comesee puts up a stop sign with her hand.

INT. BROTHER AND MARIA'S HOUSE MOMENTS

Uncle Walter's clothing is scattered throughout the room. Maria is hanging the women clothing and Brother is assembling the men's suits. He is going through the jacket pockets. He pulls out a key chain with a key on it.

BROTHER
Found an old key. What do you think it opens?

Maria continues her work and then does a double take.

MARIA
Let me see it.

Brother tosses it to her and she fondles it, flips it over and the name of first national city bank comes up.

MARIA
It's a bank key!

Brother stops hanging the suit and beckons for her to toss it back to him, she does.

BROTHER
It's a safe deposit key. Why do you think it's here?

MARIA
I don't know. Maybe he's looking for it. You think he has money?

BROTHER
You don't lose something like this.

MARIA
If he did, he would've replaced it long ago. You think its money?

BROTHER
We have money. Why are you concerned about money?

MARIA
I run this household. I was wondering how he was, or the family was going to take care of him.

Brother throws the key on the table and they both continue cleaning up.

MARIA
Are you going to tell your family about the money?

BROTHER
What money?

MARIA
Uncle Walter's.

BROTHER
It’s a key, not cash! If it was dollars, I'd have to tell them.

MARIA
Why?

BROTHER
Why are you asking? We're not hurting for money.

Brother sits and folds clothing instead of hanging them up. Maria looks away, then back at Brother. She enters his space, touches his hand showing him the clothes he should be hanging instead of folding.

MARIA
The Gillespie's have money, even us. We all doing well. Why can't we use the money for something else.

Brother stands. She touches his hand and he sits down calmly.

BROTHER
Maria, it's not our money. It’s a key and yes it’s a safe deposit box, but maybe Uncle Walter has some plans. We're not thieves.

MARIA
No one wants to keep him. We could bring my aunts and uncles here and they could take care of Uncle Walter and the

Gillespie's won't be bothered.

Brother flails his arms and stomps on the floor, as if he's having a tantrum in mime. Maria just looks at him as she continues re-doing the clothing.

BROTHER

Maria we never had a problem bringing people here. It's in the budget. Now all of a sudden new money surfaces. We don't know how much it is, and it's not ours.

MARIA

I'll talk to Uncle Walter.

Brother is surprised.

BROTHER

What sense does it make for him to use his earned money or retirement money on that idea?

MARIA

I still have the right to ask.

BROTHER

The family still has the right to know before you ask Uncle Walter.

MARIA

Why?

BROTHER

It's his money, or
I mean his key.

The sounds of children laughter in the background. He comes closer to Maria and they embrace.

BROTHER
Baby, I know your heart. We have a enough responsibilities. Uncle Walter living here full time will take away from us, the kids and both families. I'm tired.

They lightly kiss and smile at each other.

MARIA
We can't get weary in well doing.

Brother throws his hands up in the air and his head drops.

BROTHER
Where's the compromise?

MARIA
How about going to the bank first to see what we're working with?

BROTHER
I'll have to let the family know.

Maria attempts to say something in rebuttal but does not. Brother shouts out.

BROTHER
Tia I know you've been listening,

text everybody and
tell. . .

TIA
Meet you at first
national. I'll
doing it now daddy.

Brother is exhausted and shouts at Tia.

BROTHER
How? What you say
to them so quickly?

TIA
I just text money,
Uncle Walter gave
dad more for the
whole family meet
at first national
now.

Brother and Maria drop their heads. Brother leaves. Maria and Tia place the clothing in closets.

TIA
Momma, who's
clothes are these?

Tia is examining both sets of clothing.

MARIA
They're Uncle
Walter's.

Maria pauses after her statement.

TIA
But?

Maria interrupts Tia.

MARIA
I lot of his
girlfriends left
their clothes with
him when they left.

TIA

Uncle Walter was a lady's man?

MARIA
Sort of.

INT. FIRST NATIONAL BANK LOBBY-AFTERNOON

Judge, Comesee, Mm-hmm and Deuce are waiting for Brother. The normal workings of a bank are taking place. Deuce is restless, and fingering items, when someone is not tapping him he nods out. Comesee is sitting between Judge and Mm-hmm who are ignoring each other, both are talking to Comesee. Deuce chimes in every now and then.

COMESEE
Me and Mm-hmm were talking about how we can help Brother.

MM-HMM
Especially, if he's taking on Uncle Walter, with Maria and three kids.

Judge turns her head to face Mm-hmm and Comesee, but looks at Comesee.

JUDGE
And.

MM-HMM
Yes, this involves you.

Deuce gets up and starts playing with deposit slips and points at customers like he knows them. Mm-hmm snatches him down to a seat. The sound makes a noise and everyone else semi-looks in their direction.

JUDGE

You people are embarrassing me.

Mm-hmm raises from her chair pulling off her earrings but looks around and stops. Comesee touches Mm-hmm arm and she remains seated.

COMESEE

Girl, we are your people, you can't change us.

DEUCE

Why is Brother in charge of Uncle Walter's money? He only wants him for a month. I want him to live with me.

COMESEE/JUDGE/MM-HMM

Where?

DEUCE

That's beside the point.

JUDGE

Perhaps there's a large sum of money.

MM-HMM

So are you saying, you're better qualified to manage it? I manage thousands of grant money at community center that your firm of liars, I mean lawyers own.

JUDGE

Lower you voice, I'm not going there with you right now, but soon.

Judge points her fingers at Mm-hmm. Mm-hmm snaps two fingers back at her.

COMESEE
None of us need the money. We're just thinking about Brother and the weight he's carrying with these decisions.

DEUCE
I'll take it from him. I know a rehab clinic. They could get me off heroin and get me on methadone.

The ladies refuse to comment.

DEUCE
Why is everybody looking at me that way?

Deuce starts to scratch himself all over. A bank employee comes over.

BANK EMPLOYEE
Excuse me folks, I notice you been sitting for a while, can I be of service?

Judge changes her demeanor and voice tone.

JUDGE
Yes, well, I'm the family attorney and we're waiting on another family member so we can

conduct some
business here.

BANK EMPLOYEE

Well, it seems the
hour is running
behind, I've notice
everyone been here
quite some time.

He eyeballs Deuce suspiciously because of his movements, nodding, loud voice, and playing with materials.

JUDGE

He'll be here.

BANK EMPLOYEE

Does anyone have an
account with us?

Everyone freezes.

DEUCE

I'll open one.

Bank employee looks at him and ignores him.

BANK EMPLOYEE

We have a policy
that prohibits
individuals from
waiting for
customers that
aren't here.

COMESEE

The woman said the
man will be here.
Now go get us a
toaster or
something. The man
said he wants to
open an account.

The bank employee walks away dejected and embarrassed. Brother walks into the bank. They all rush up to him.

MM-HMM

Where have you been? They are just about to call security on us.

Brother looks around at people staring at them. Deuce is nodding in the chair.

BROTHER
Why yawl bring him to a bank dressed like that?

The sound of Brother's voice jars Deuce.

DEUCE
I heard that.

JUDGE
Did Uncle Walter send some money to take care of his daily expenses?

COMESEE
How are we going to send it to everyone on a month to month basis?

MM-HMM
It would be better if everyone received a check and not cash. It could be mismanaged. I could help in its allocation.

DEUCE
Why are you always in charge? Uncle Walter doesn't even know you.

Brother stares down Deuce. Deuce ignores it.

BROTHER
Does anybody know him?

DEUCE
That's beside the point.

Brother shakes his head.

JUDGE
Are you going to deposit the check in a checking or saving account CD or what?

BROTHER
What is everyone talking about? All I have is a key.

COMESEE
Keys? What are you talking about?

BROTHER
What else did Tia text to you? All I found was a safe deposit box key.

MM-HMM
Uncle Walter showed wisdom, leaving valuables in a safe deposit box.

DEUCE
What are you waiting for? We need somebody else in charge of Uncle Walter. You're too slow for me. You're late too. Why are

you just standing
there?

Brother's angry. The bank manager comes over.

BANK MANAGER
Excuse me folks,
can I help? Is
there a problem?

BROTHER
No sir, no problem.
I would like to
open the box this
key belongs to.

He hands the key to the bank manager who examines it, then looks at everyone.

BANK MANAGER
Sir, if you would
accompany me to my
desk then we should
be able to help you
and your friends.

Brother follows the manager to his back room office. The manager offers Brother a seat in front of his desk and he sits in one facing Brother. He continues examining the key.

BANK MANAGER
How long have you
had this key?

BROTHER
It belongs to our
Uncle.

BANK MANAGER
Oh, it's not yours?

BROTHER
No, it's our
Uncle's

BANK MANAGER

We actually don't use this system anymore. We revamped our entire system. I've only seen this key in our archives.

BROTHER
What are you saying?

BANK MANAGER
We're not using literal keys or cards anymore. We use the retina of the eyes to open the safe squares.

BROTHER
Safe squares?

BANK MANAGER
Safe deposit boxes are such an ancient name. We banned it long ago. Just have your Uncle drop by and it shouldn't take long.

Brother sits on the edge of his seat.

BROTHER
He's in a nursing home . . . But we'll be picking him up this weekend. Is there anything I can do now because he may need some money?

BANK MANAGER
Certainly, if you have power of attorney over your

Uncle’s finances then we can have your retina verified.

Brother grabs a pad and pen from the manager's desk.

BROTHER

Please tell me again what I need from my Uncle.

Brother writes down information.

BANK MANAGER

I'll provide you with the printout version for what you need.

From below the bank manager’s desk the documents arrive. Brother briefly scans it. The bank manager stands which forces Brother to stand and he extends his hand. He escorts him to the door.

BROTHER

Excuse me, is there another way out of here, without going back through the lobby?

Bank manager unlocks side door and lets him out. Brother walks to his car. He drives by the front of the building. Judge, Deuce, and Mm-hmm are standing near the door and see his car go by. They all look at each other and jet out the door. Comesee embarrassed, runs out also.

INT/EXT. JUDGE'S CAR MOMENTS LATER

Judge's is driving fast weaving in and out of traffic. She is barely keeping up with

Brother. He doesn't know they are behind him. Deuce is in the front seat.

JUDGE
Deuce stop touching stuff. All of these things were custom made for me.

Deuce continues to touch the console, glove box, as if a child was investigating a new toy.

DEUCE
How long have you had this car?

JUDGE
Just as long as you've been gone. I'm trying to keep it clean, so stop touching stuff.

DEUCE
When are you going let me drive it? I'm your brother.

Judge, still manipulates through traffic, laughs almost to tears, then immediately becomes stoic.

JUDGE
You must be joking. How or why would I let you drive my car? Did you shower this morning?

DEUCE
Light.

JUDGE
Light? What's a light shower? You need hard and long showers.

Deuce shouts at Judge.

DEUCE
No, red light!

Judge jams on her breaks in the middle of intersection. Brother's truck has crossed over and gone ahead.

DEUCE
I saved your life.

Judge angrily motions for Deuce to get in the backseat. He does so with his butt high up in the air bumping her. Judge gets a stench. She covers her nose. The light changes and she zooms across.

JUDGE
You better learn how to wipe!

Brother is clueless. He smells his hands and shrugs his shoulders.

JUDGE
Look, before we get to Brother's house, I need you to back me on an idea I had.

Deuce is relaxing in the back seat. Judge watches him from the rear view mirror. He begins to scratch himself.

JUDGE
Do whatever you have to do to stay awake, just don't nod out.

DEUCE
So what if I did? You ain't going to bust me.

JUDGE

I just don't want to get stopped and some cop searching you and my Beemer.

DEUCE

I think you want to get stopped, so you can see how your brother survives.

JUDGE

Why would I want to get stopped?

DEUCE

You just left a bank in a hurry, in a fast car chasing another car, stopped in the middle of a crossroads and you're speeding.

Judge slows down and blends in with traffic. Deuce scoots over so that he's directly behind the passenger seat and Judge can see half his face in the rearview mirror.

JUDGE

I lost Brother in this traffic. You know where he lives.

DEUCE

Sure do, but you can wave Mm-hmm on. I know she behind you.

JUDGE

Why should I do that when you can lead me there? I thought you knew how to get there. I really don't want to ask her nothing. I need your backing on something else.

DEUCE
I only know the way by walking. I don't know it by car. Just wave her around.

Reluctantly, she waves Mm-hmm car around. Mm-hmm car passes Judge's car and neither driver look at each other. Mm-hmm waves in Deuce's direction.

DEUCE
Why you two have so much beef?

JUDGE
Why, what she say?

DEUCE
My name is Bennett I ain't in it.

JUDGE
Let me tell you what I've been doing for the family.

Deuce sits back and with his hand behind the driver's seat, he places refer paper on his knee, and pulls out marijuana and rolls it up. Leans his head out of view and licks the joint and puts it in his mouth.

JUDGE
I've arranged for everybody to have Uncle Walter go to different locations during their month.

Deuce clears his throat as he put away his stash and pulls out his lighter.

DEUCE
What you talking about? He's staying with me.

JUDGE
Just hear me out. I've got access to YMCA, spas, hotels, cruises, hostels and shelters that we can use for a month.

DEUCE
Make a left here. I know that church.

JUDGE
What do you know about a church?

DEUCE
It's the only one surrounded by liquor stores.

Judge looks out the window and sees what Deuce described and also real estate signs with her picture and law firm.

JUDGE
What you think of my proposal?

DEUCE
I ain't marrying nobody.

JUDGE
Ain't no body marrying me either, fool. I'm talking about my idea.

DEUCE
Sounds like you should have hooked me up a long time ago.

JUDGE
I can't, cause you dealing with that addiction.

Deuce sits back, hits the lighter and flames the joint. Judge is furious as she weaves her head back in forth in the rearview mirror.

DEUCE
What addiction?

JUDGE
Tell me you not smoking in my car. I just had the ash trays removed so nobody would smoke.

DEUCE
There won't be no ashes.

Judge deeply inhales to offset her frustration.

DEUCE
Be careful girl.

JUDGE
Is that crack! Oh my Lord, I've got crack in my car!

DEUCE
Calm down Judge, crack stinks. I've

got my pride. I
don't do that new
stuff. I'm old
school. This just a
little mary-jane.

Judge puts her sunglasses on and scoots down lower in the driver's seat.

JUDGE
Why are you doing
this to me? I just
want to get to
Brother's safely
and no problems.

DEUCE
Can't a man get his
head right?

He leans back and smokes comfortably as if he's alone on a beach. Deuce keeps smoking occasional, blowing the smoke in her direction. She lets the window down quickly.

DEUCE
You might want to
let it up a lot
more, this smoke is
heavier and might
cause somebody to
get a contact.

JUDGE
We could get
arrested.

Deuce laughs. She quickly let’s her window up.

DEUCE
Are you saying,
Uncle Walt is going
to be staying at
those places?

JUDGE
Yes.

DEUCE
When everybody going to see him?

JUDGE
When it's our time to pick him up and take him to wherever he's going to stay for that month.

DEUCE
Who's paying for this?

JUDGE
We all do, except you and he could use his own money to do what he wants. Whoever has him that month could help him manage his money.

Deuce takes some more puffs. He looks at the joint admirably. Speaking while holding smoke in.

DEUCE
Uncle Walt is like this joint. Some people curious, some want to keep it, and some want to get rid of it. It's got a purpose. They say its Metamucil like that cereal, which it's good for you.

JUDGE
You mean medicinal purposes.

DEUCE

Yeah, now you understand what I'm saying.

JUDGE

Actually, I don't. I just want you out of the car and some rational conversation. I just can't reason with you.

DEUCE

Sorry, I'll break it down for you. You're so educated you forgot what you're suppose to remember.

JUDGE

Please enlighten me.

DEUCE

All of us need Uncle Walt and he needs us.

Judge makes a left turn still looking for familiar landmarks.

JUDGE

Praise God, we're getting close to Brother's place.

DEUCE

We don't have any seniors in this family. The oldest is Mm-hmm, and you two fight. She's like an older sister more than anything.

JUDGE

I'll rent some seniors if I need sage advice.

DEUCE
They won't be family!

JUDGE
He's family but he's not family.

He exhales smoke as he leans forward behind Judge's ear.

DEUCE
That's daddy's brother.

JUDGE
Why do have to go there? I miss him so much.

DEUCE
I talk to God. He told me our daddy missed his brother. All the brothers use to constantly look for him. How you think Brother got his name?

Judge follows Mm-hmm car to the back of the house. Brother's car is not there. Comesee's car comes from the opposite direction. Comesee and Mm-hmm exit the car and knock on the door and no one answers. They sit in the swing in the backyard.

JUDGE
I just don't think we could all deal with Uncle on a full time or monthly basis. The money is not

problem, it's the time.

DEUCE

How you think daddy would feel if he knew the next set of kids found his brother and we passed him on because we didn't know him?

JUDGE

You talk to God about your addiction?

Deuce is uncomfortable with the question. He puts the joint out on his blistered palm.

DEUCE

Yeah.

JUDGE

What did he say?

DEUCE

I have to wait till I come off this high to understand. He called me Gomer.

JUDGE

I just don't understand you. Come on let's get out before they start thinking we're being antisocial.

EXT.OUTSIDE CAR BROTHER'S HOUSE BACKYARD.

They exit the smoke filled car. Mm-hmm and Comesee just scream in laughter. Deuce speaks to Judge, though she ignores him.

DEUCE

How come our family can’t deal with Uncle Walt, but yawl can deal with me?

INT. BELAIR NURSING HOME DAY

Brother is standing at the front desk. CARMEN the front desk clerk hands him paper work. He fills it out. She leaves the desk.

CARMEN

Sir you can follow me. Most of the clients are in the day room. You can fill those papers out there with your uncle.

Brother nods and follows her. He walks peeping in and out of doorways, before he's noticed. He quickens his steps behind Carmen. He doesn't want to make his face obvious.

Carmen points to a large room full of seniors and she motions for Brother. He grabs a wall and slides in without disturbing the bingo game.

CARMEN

We have three Walters here. One of them is in here. Do you see him?

Brother scans the room, but he also scans Carmen point of view. Carmen points in far corner. An elderly gentleman is playing a game of chess with another resident. Carmen tugs Brother and he follows making haste trying to see the client before she gets to him. He's weaving in and out of residents.

CARMEN

Mr. Walter there's someone here to see you.

Mr. Walter looks up from his game as well as the other resident. Brother extends his hand for a handshake. Mr. Walter attempts to stand but is unable to. Carmen makes him sit.

CARMEN

Mr. Walter, your family member is here.

Again Brother extends his hand and Mr. Walter grabs at the air and Brother directs his hands to Mr. Walter's.

BROTHER

Hi Uncle Walter, how are you?

Mr. Walter releases Brother's hand quick as if it had something on it. Carmen consoles the senior.

CARMEN

Is everything ok Mr. Walter?

He goes back to the chess board reaching for a piece on the board.

MR. WALTER

My daughter's voice doesn't sound like that.

Carmen smiles, and nudges Brother to say something.

BROTHER

It's your nephew Uncle Walter, I was checking on you.

Mr. Walter franticly shakes his head, several times. He stands and swings a fist aimlessly at Brother. Carmen puts her hand on his shoulder and whispers in his ear. She touches Brother's shoulder and they walk away.

BROTHER
What did you say to him?

CARMEN
I asked him to be nice when we have company. When was the last time you saw your Uncle?

BROTHER
It's been a while.

Brother avoids eye contact with Carmen. Brother looks around at other residents. Carmen watches his point of view.

CARMEN
We get that a lot. Most drop them off and never see them again.

Carmen lightly elbows Brother to look out the far window and watch the mass exodus of family members dropping residents. He sadly turns away.

BROTHER
You said there were three Walters here.

CARMEN
Now there's two left. I don't think he was your Uncle.

Brother looks at her than at another Mr. Walter that Carmen points toward.

BROTHER

What makes you
think he's not my
Uncle?

CARMEN
You would have
known he's been
blind all his life.

Carmen slaps her forehead and walks to the front desk. Brother follows her. She checks the files.

CARMEN
Is there anything
wrong with your
Uncle? Why is he
here?

BROTHER
We are suppose to
pick him up this
weekend. Why did
you ask about my
Uncle's health?

Carmen goes to another file cabinet and pulls out several files but returns them.

CARMEN
You didn't bring
Mr. Walter here,
did you?

Brother slightly backs up toward the front door, looking up the hallways for security.

BROTHER
I think I should
go.

Carmen closes the file cabinet. She exits the main room and heads down the hall.

CARMEN
Please wait here.
We have some
records in the
other building.

Brother seizes the opportunity and zooms for the door. He sees an older woman peep out of her room and gesture for him to come toward her. She looks for anyone. Everyone is occupied. He walks over.

BROTHER
Hi, I really have to leave. The lady will be back soon. She'll help you.

ELSIE
The name's Elsie. Who you looking for?

She slips out of her bedroom. She motions him to come closer. They stand in a shadow of a corridor.

ELSIE
Who you looking for? She don't know jack. I've been here since first light.

She adjusts her wig all the way around. Brother moves closer to hear her. She grabs her walker and nods her head for Brother to follow. They walk through another door.

BROTHER
I'm looking for Walter Gillespie. Do you know him? He's my Uncle.

Elsie turns her back to him, grabs her walker and step by step walks through a door. Brother follows. The door slams as Brother hears the sound of rumbling feet.

BROTHER

Is this the only way out of here?

Elsie stops her walker and methodically turns to Brother.

ELSIE

These young people are in so much of a hurry. Don't you want to see your Uncle?

Brother nods his head and she continues her walk down a long hallway. The clink of her walker hitting the floor is heard. Brother is close behind her walking at a snail pace. He is also looking back for security to approach.

BROTHER

Can you tell me something, anything about my Uncle? I haven't seen him for in a long time.

Again Elsie stops her walker, turns and looks at Brother.

ELSIE

You're making me tired. Do you want to talk or walk? You young people don't know how to make a decision.

BROTHER

OK, sorry.

Brother tries to usher her forward. He gets in front of her, instead of behind her, edging her on faster.

Elsie's walker clicks and clacks. Brother is walking backwards facing the doorway but in front of Elsie walking space. She stops again. Brother drops his head because she stopped.

BROTHER
What's wrong? Are you ok? Are you tired?

Elsie shakes her head no to his questions.

ELSIE
You're in my way.

She pushes him out of the way and continues down the tinged yellow hallway of apartments/home.

They are halfway down the hallway and security enters the same corridor. They walk in the same direction but don't notice him from a distance. Carmen is not with them. They are checking the doors, yet heading in their direction.

BROTHER
Can I do anything to help you?

Elsie again stops her walker with a sudden jump.

ELSIE
Are we talking or walking?

Brother looks at security coming closer. He kneels down on one knee and unties his shoes and slowly reties them. His head is downward.

BROTHER
Ah, we're talking.

Elsie scoots herself over to the edge of the windows. She props herself against it watching Brother tightening his shoe strings.

I/E. BROTHER'S BACK PORCH-DAY

Mm-hmm, Deuce, Comesee and Judge are playing spades. Deuce is shuffling and dealing the cards. Judge and Mm-hmm avoid eye contact. They are talking around each other.

Everyone has picked up their cards and assembling them in order. Deuce hand signals and gestures over the table to Mm-hmm. Comesee does the same to Judge. Everyone enjoys the moment.

COMESEE

In all these years, all of us still cheat at cards.

MM-HMM

Some of us don't want to let it go.

Judge glances at Mm-hmm. She doesn't return the stare. They play another hand and Comesee and Judge win.

JUDGE

Just like old times girl, we always were better. Remember after we graduated high school.

COMESEE

Yep, we had that party, and came home late.

JUDGE

We got in trouble, but our parents were cool. They knew I was college bound.

COMESEE

They knew me and Basil was getting married.

JUDGE
I can't believe you and Basil been married since after high school.

Deuce and Mm-hmm look at each other as cards are being dealt.

MM-HMM
Can we talk about something else besides high school dreams?

COMESEE
Some people loved life after high school.

JUDGE
Yep.

Mm-hmm looks harshly at Judge.

MM-HMM
What are you getting at?

Judge holds her hands up in the air and looks at everyone.

JUDGE
It's your deal, not mine.

Mm-hmm grabs the cards and shuffles quick, then deals cards from left to right and Judge gets the last hand.

DEUCE
Misdeal, misdeal. Dealer gets the

last hand. Deal
right Mm-hmm!

Everyone throws cards back on the table. Mm-hmm deals correctly. Players pick up their cards.

MM-HMM
I do the right
thing. Everybody
doesn't deal right.

DEUCE
What are you
talking about?

Everyone places the cards on the table.

COMESEE
You two are dulling
the game. What's
the deal with you
two?

Judge picks up her cards and shuffles with all kinds of card tricks.

JUDGE
I learned this also
in law school.

Judge deals hands quickly. She slides the cards across the table each time she slides them it speeds up and the players have to grab it before it goes off the table. She shoots one and two at Mm-hmm. It slides off the table. Deuce picks it up, peeps at it and then gives it to Mm-hmm.

MM-HMM
Why do you keep
doing that?

For the first time they both look at each other rather rough.

JUDGE
It because you
can't deal, or

don't know how to
deal.

MM-HMM
I've been dealing
all my life, you
had all the cards.

The game begins as they talk over the table.

JUDGE
After graduation,
we all had the same
hand.

Comesee looks inside the house window back and forth from her seat.

COMESEE
Why do you think
Brother is not here
yet?

Deuce gets up and walks around the front of the house. He returns.

DEUCE
He better not spend
any of Uncle's
money.

Mm-hmm plays her hand first. Comesee and Deuce add to the cards. Judge slams her card on top of the others.

JUDGE
I don't have no
regrets about what
I played. Some
people like to
renege and wish
they had a better
hand.

COMESEE
We forgot to bid on
the books. We'll
take 6 books.

MM-HMM
You sure look like a blind to me.

DEUCE
We'll take what's left.

Judge stands up and looks down at Mm-hmm, who also stands. They lean across the table face to face.

JUDGE
You're so bitter.

She shakes her head and sits down. Mm-hmm does the same.

MM-HMM
You're so ungrateful.

JUDGE
You just want to be me. You should have taken the LSAT till you passed it.

MM-HMM
Everybody couldn't afford the prep course.

JUDGE
You're a community activist. You're making a difference with the people.

Comesee and Deuce pack the cards up and close up the card table.

MM-HMM
You are liar and not a lawyer.

JUDGE
They gave me an offer. I had to butter bagels.

DEUCE
This ain't about neither one of you, it's about Uncle Walt.

COMESEE
You both need to shut up and get over that old hurt. You making it new again. Both of you screwed up the game.

Deuce enters Judge's car. She takes notice and heads down the stairs toward him. She shouts.

JUDGE
Why are you in my car?

Deuce emerges with his hand up holding her cell phone.

DEUCE
I was calling Brother, your judgeship.

She opens all the doors and fans the stale smoke out of the car and places her items back in her purse that Deuce rumbled through. She turns to him and snatches her phone from him.

INT. BELAIR NURSING HOME-HALLWAY-DAY

Brother finished tying his shoes and security has walked by. Elsie continues up the hall. Brother motions her to move faster. She pushes him to the side. Brother's phone startles her and he quickly quiets it but drops it. Elsie stops again and pauses to breath.

ELSIE
This hallway looks
longer.

BROTHER
It's a little
further.

Brother jumps at any sounds. Elsie points further down the hall.

ELSIE
Your uncle lives
down there.

Brother looks at her. Elsie breathes heavy.

BROTHER
Are you going to be
OK?

Elsie motions with two fingers as if she's smoking a cigarette.

BROTHER
Too many, huh?

ELSIE
I need one plus
some oxygen.

Brother continues walking and looks back at Elsie. She waves and shakes her head. He shouts back.

BROTHER
What will I do if
security comes
back?

Elsie puts her mouth between her hands and shouts back.

ELSIE
You had better
think of something.
They are coming
now.

Security is walking rapidly toward him. He walks toward them at the same pace. They slow down and angle toward him, but Brother continues. They meet head on. He points toward Elsie.

BROTHER
My mom, she needs oxygen. I'll be right back. Please watch her.

They run toward her to comfort her as Brother continues to the hallway door. He enters a door with a dreary contrast to the nursing home.

INT. BELAIR FUNERAL HOME-MOMENTS LATER

Brother walks through a parlor full of empty coffins. Curtains are gone between viewing rooms. There is an office where he hears voices. The door is ajar and he lightly knocks and enters. The two occupants are sitting in wheeled chairs sweeping.

Fern

Come in.

She looks at Dern and shrugs her shoulders.

FERN
You expecting company?

Dern shakes his head no, and rises to meet Brother.

BROTHER
Hi, I was told my uncle was living over here. Does he work here?

FERN

What's his name?
I'll have to see.

Dern shrugs his shoulders, then nudges his sister and points at himself and her.

FERN
Oh. We're the only ones that work here.

Brother observes the place.

BROTHER
Is this a part of the nursing home?

DERN
It used to be. We're closing.

FERN
For good. Who's your family?

Brother turns to leave.

FERN
Be careful heading back, security was just here. They're looking for a guy.

Brother turns back to them.

BROTHER
You wouldn't happen to have any oxygen, cigarettes or an exit.

Brother pushes the trash away and picks up a booklet of the Funeral home.

BROTHER

Is this really a
Funeral home?

DERN
Not anymore.

Dern points toward an exit and Brother follows the directions.

FERN
Where's you're
uncle?

BROTHER
Where's the Jane?

Dern walks Brother to the bathroom.

DERN
Someone said you're
uncle lives and
works here?

Fern stands and quickly cleans up while talking.

FERN
Your uncle's name
ain't Bill-lee is
it?

Brother yawns.

BROTHER
Gillespie, is his
last name, Walter
is his first.

Fern and Dern look at each other, then at Brother. Then they start cleaning the office as if a question wasn't asked.

BROTHER
You know him?

Fern shakes her head yes while Dern shakes his head no. Once they see each other's reaction they reverse the action.

FERN
Who sent you here?

Brother measures the height and weight of Elsie and mimics her walking with the walker, pointing in Elsie's direction.

BROTHER
Her name is Elsie. She said my uncle lives here.

DERN
You mean a short tall lady, built sort of round and square, who won't let you talk till she finished walking.

FERN
She wears a night gown, during the day and she likes oxygen and smokes?

Brother nods and smiles in agreement.

BROTHER
So you know her?

FERN/DERN
No.

The twins walk toward Brother and try to usher him out of the room. Fern hits a light switch. Dern is sweeping faster and Brother is walking backwards toward the exit door. Brother reacts and pushes Dern backwards. Dern shoves Brother.

BROTHER
What's the rush.

FERN
You're not suppose to be in here.

Brother's phone rings. It startles him and it takes him a minute to find it. He answers it while looking at Fern and Dern, who are preparing him to leave. He answers the phone but he missed the call.

EXT. BROTHER'S BACKYARD PORCH-MOMENTS-LATER

COMESEE
You two call him,
and we'll text him.

Deuce is standing behind everyone and scratching on the porch. The ladies are sitting on the edge of the porch. Deuce goes to the back door and is silently breaking the seal on the window. Mm-hmm glances back and Deuce freezes then she looks away. Deuce breaks the door knob, while the ladies are phoning other numbers to reach Brother. Judge catches Deuce.

JUDGE
I'm not bailing
you.

The other women see the damage he's done. They hang up the phones. Deuce continues scratching as a diversion to what he's done.

DEUCE
I have to get
inside. Brother's
taking too long. I
need to speak to
Uncle Walter.

The women examine the damage that's been done.

JUDGE
Are you still
trying to get me
arrested?

DEUCE
I could still get us in if you'll let me finish. It's just the back door.

The ladies push Deuce away from the house. They sit him down on the steps. He is scratching his body harder. He is frantic and can't sit still.

DEUCE
Why he ain't here yet? Why Maria not home or the kids? We need to get inside. They stole the money.

He starts for the house again but the women block him and he stands in the yard. He paces north and south. He grabs a branch and runs toward them. They scatter and he angles toward the house window. Mm-hmm trips him from running up the stairs and he loses his balance and stick.

JUDGE
Deuce you need some help. I didn't know you were this bad.

Deuce looks at her then her car. She looks for her purse on the porch. Deuce eyes that.

DEUCE
What do you want me to say?

COMESEE
A sorry would help.

DEUCE
Sorry, but I need some dollars.

MM-HMM
You can't give a junkie nothing.

COMESEE
Deuce's two days are running out.

JUDGE
Where's does he go to get his stuff?

Mm-hmm walks shaking her head and waves her hand Judge.

COMESEE
The same places that your firm owns and are trying to redevelop and move people out.

Judge points at Deuce who is on the ground rolling back and forth in the dirt screaming and scratching his body. He jumps up and runs toward Mm-hmm. She grabs a shovel and swings at him. She misses the first time but he tries to grab her purse. She hits him broad side with the shovel and both falls to the ground. Comesee and Mm-hmm sit on top of his back.

DEUCE
Judge, you can get me in a program, help me.

Deuce rolls them over. He's on his knees and climbs the top step. He grabs Judge's keys and jumps up and runs for the car. Comesee trips him and he falls hard on some isolated concrete. He breaks a tooth and is bleeding. Judge panics and she hurries herself to help him.

JUDGE

He's bleeding. We can't wait on Brother.

Comesee and Mm-hmm don't react. They just keep eyeing Deuce.

DEUCE

Does anybody have any ice?

He wipes his mouth with his sleeve but blood drips fast.

MM-HMM

If we had ice, do you think we'd be outside?

DEUCE

Can somebody drop me off at the icehouse?

Deuce walks out of the backyard to the front entrance. The women follow him. He knocks and no response. He tries to unlock it. He looks in both directions and starts in one way. Then turns around and walks in opposite direction. Judge tackles him on the grass.

MM-HMM

What are you doing girl?

Neighbors are looking around as Judge and Deuce wrestle on the lawn. Comesee and Mm-hmm referee.

DEUCE

I have to go.

COMESEE

Let that man-child go. We can't compete with heroin.

INT. BELAIR FUNERAL HOME MOMENTS-LATER

Fern and Dern are facing Brother at the exit. There is a sudden knock at the door, which frightens all of them. No one moves. They knock again. Brother recoups to slide behind Fern and Dern who are backing up simultaneously. Brother still remains in front. Fern salutes her finger over her mouth for silence. Dern whisper's to Brother.

DERN
You expecting
anybody?

Fern shoves Dern. Brother holds up both his hands in disbelief. Fern whispers.

FERN
There's not suppose
to be any bodies
here.

Everyone backs up, the knock threaten's their ears. Fern bumps into a chair. Fern and Dern nod to Brother to open it. Brother skims their faces. He twist the handle, looks down and sees a shadow underneath. Brother glances back at Fern and Dern and they've vanished. He swirls in all directions and only hallway dust is flying around. Brother whispers to the door.

BROTHER
There's nobody
here.

Brother smacks his forehead. The knock jars the door. Brother sighs and drops to the floor and cracks the door and peeps upward. The door slams open and hits Brother in the head and someone peeks around the door.

ELSIE
What are you doing
on the floor?

Elsie muscles her walker in. Brother rolls over holding his head. He observes behind her and shuts the door.

ELSIE

How much you think these depends can hold? I have to pee.

She goes to the bathroom. Brother sits up holding his head. Elsie emerges and Brother stands.

ELSIE

Did you find him?

Brother shakes his head no. Elsie shakes her head no and waves for Brother to follow her again. They exit the door she came through.

INT. A WALKTHROUGH LAUNDRY ROOM.

In the all white painted laundry room, a couple of residents are washing clothing. They eye the Brother and Elsie as they shuffle through to the other side.

INT. A RESIDENT'S ROOM MOMENTS-LATER

Elsie remains staying near the door but has not entered. She knocks. There is some rumbling of the bed and sheets. She nods for Brother to go ahead of her. He walks in on a senior couple half-dressed on the bed kissing. The woman's back is to Brother and the man sees Brother enter.

BROTHER

Oh! Excuse me. I didn't mean.

The man kisses the woman and waves for Brother to stay. The woman turns over and he spoons her. Brother takes a step back and bumps into a chair.

BROTHER

Hi, I'm looking for
my Uncle Walter.

The senior couple look at each other, then at Brother.

BROTHER

I'm sorry, I came
at the wrong time.

The couple nod their heads in agreement and Brother drops his head.

WALTER-LEE

My name is Walter-
Lee I don't
remember having a
nephew, which side
were you on?

BROTHER

You've got several
nieces and nephews
on your brother's
side.

Walter-Lee uncovers himself, adjust himself, covers the lady, gets out of bed and walks over to Brother and extends his hand.

WALTER-LEE

Well hello nephew,
what's your name?

Brother starts backing up and doesn't shake his hand. Walter-Lee looks at his hands, wipes them off and then extends them to Brother. Brother shakes his hand but heads for the door again bumping into the chair. Elsie is outside the door.

BROTHER

I'm sorry, there's
been a mistake. I
kind of wish you
were my uncle.

You're smooth, but
you're not him. I'm
sorry.

Brother exits, Walter-Lee shrugs and runs toward the bed. There is aged laughter between the couple.

I/E. OUTSIDE WALTER-LEE'S ROOM-MOMENTS LATER

Brother wrestle for a deep breath and ganders a shadow, a thin line of smoke trailing upward and a tank of oxygen along and cannula in Elsie's nose. She tilts toward him and gives him a thumbs up. He mocks her with a thumbs down. Brother walks in the direction of scattered voices.

ELSIE

Psst, psst.

Brother looks back, without stopping. Elsie takes a mammoth inhale of oxygen and cigarette.

ELSIE

There's still
another Walter.

Brother does a three sixty and holds his arms up in the air with desperation. Elsie shouts back.

ELSIE

How did you know it
wasn't him?

Brother flees and doesn't hear her question. Elsie nails another hit of the oxygen and cigarette. She meddles in another client's room who is sleeping and replaces the pack and oxygen and slides the door.

Elsie cross the hall and knocks on the door twice. Walter comes to the door out of breath and sweating.

WALTER-LEE

Yes, yes what is it?

Elsie, almost falls back but catches herself on her walker. Walter-Lee has dwarfism.

EXT. BROTHER'S HOUSE FRONT LAWN-LATER

Deuce jolts Judge off his back. The women try to grab him. He tears off down the road running out of his shirt. A car nearly pummels him. The women sit on the grass. All their clothes are tattered. Comesee looks at Judge then starts laughing and Mm-hmm chimes in.

Judge shocked at their laughter and notice's they are laughing at her. They point to the real estate sign 90 feet in the air of Judge. She looks up at herself then down at her current condition. She begins laughing at herself also. Brother drives up. He smiles searching for the joke.

BROTHER

Hey, sorry I'm late. I had to check in with Maria and the kids, and I'll fill you in.

Brother walks toward the front entrance, then double-takes the ladies.

BROTHER

Why yawl not inside?

He notices his house is closed up and he opens it and invites them in. The women gather their things and quickly assemble around Brother.

COMESEE

How are you Brother of mine?

She tries to hug him but he takes her arms from around his neck and points to a picture of Maria and shows them his wedding band (smiling)as he scours the house for his family.

BROTHER
What time is it?

Judge checks her watch and shakes it hard and listens to it and its obvious it’s broken. Mm-hmm checks her cell but doesn't say anything about the time.

MM-HMM
Don't you have clocks in your house.

Brother smacks his forehead, and jets to poolroom. He slaps himself again and rushes for the front door. The women parachute out of the way.

JUDGE
Where are you going, we need to talk.

Brother jumps back in his truck.

BROTHER
I forgot to get the kids and tonight's class night. I'll try and meet Maria. It’s obvious where she is.

They hole up their hands wondering what Brother is referring Brother searches around them.

BROTHER
Where's the family dope fein?

Everyone mediates on Brother driving away. Comesee observes the school buses and kids walking home. She waves and jumps in her car and zooms off. Judge is still sitting on the grass. Mm-hmm offers her hand to help her up but Judge refuses it.

She limps with a broken heel to the steps. Mm-hmm walks beside her and they enter Brother's house.

INT. BROTHER AND MARIA'S HOUSE MOMENTS LATER

MM-HMM
Look I really have to go.

Judge continues fixing her heel, which doesn't work. She packs her stuff also and heads for the door.

MM-HMM
Where are you going?

JUDGE
My job is done.

MM-HMM
We both can't leave.

Mm-hmm goes to the back door and pulls the door from the inside and it opens and the lock is broken then she opens and closes the front door.

JUDGE
Brother left us no key. You should stay.

MM-HMM
Sorry, I can't.

Both rush for the door and reach the doorway at the same time with their gear in tow and crash into each other knocking their butts to the floor. They laugh. Judge stands and offers help, but Mm-hmm refuses and stands.

Judge closes the door and walks back to the kitchen and Mm-hmm follows.

INT. BROTHER AND MARIA'S KITCHEN-MOMENTS LATER

Mm-hmm wades at the kitchen table and spreads the daily newspaper across the table. Judge snatches a wash towel and washes her face in the kitchen sink then places the towel back. She secures two slices of bread and makes one sandwich. She sits down at the table with minimum place for her meal and drink.

MM-HMM
Thank you.

Judge rolls her eyes and studies Mm-hmm newspaper upside down. She reaches for an unread section and Mm-hmm picks it up to read it.

JUDGE
One thing about you Mm-hmm, you won't sugar coat nothing about me.

MM-HMM
You got that right.

JUDGE
What you think about the family shipping Uncle Walter to a resort, hotel, spa each month?

Mm-hmm emerges from the table, takes her paper under her arm, opens a can of soup, pours it in a bowl and tosses it in the microwave. Judge watches the paper. She spreads her sandwich and drink further away from her.

MM-HMM
Who thought of that?

JUDGE
I did. We do business travel all the time.

Mm-hmm makes herself an identical sandwich and drink.

MM-HMM
Does this excuse you from your monthly Uncle Walter visit?

JUDGE
I'm the coordinator of this event. We work with these companies all the time without my influences.

The microwave dings. Mm-hmm semi-slams her soup-bowl on the table. Some of the drink splashes on Judges face. She methodically wipes it off with her sleeve. Mm-hmm places her paper back on the table and nods at Judge to move her items. Judge doesn't move anything.

MM-HMM
You're a control freak.

JUDGE
Me? How come no man want's to stay with you.

Judge takes a bite of her sandwich and chews angrily.

MM-HMM
I know you don't want to go there!

Judge throws up her hands, stands and wields her earrings off and shoves the chair back, which falls over. Mm-hmm laughs at her, remaining in her seat.

JUDGE
What are you trying to say about my selection of men?

Judge circles Mm-hmm, sizing her up. Mm-hmm just ignores her and laughs. Judge slams her hand on the table and breaks a nail. She comforts herself.

JUDGE
I have to make a nail appointment.

MM-HMM
How is www.losers.com?

Judge quickly sits trounced. Mm-hmm sips her soup and dips her sandwich inside soup.

JUDGE
That's nasty.

MM-HMM
What's nasty is you dating those dope boys?

Judge starts eating rather fast.

JUDGE
Those are the only guys I attract and at least I attract some.

Mm-hmm doesn't react.

MM-HMM

Maybe you should
change your
hairstyle. It's a
little too street.

Judge fingers her hair and picks up a ladle and looks at her reflection.

JUDGE
The last time I
changed styles, I
was attracting
Momma's boys and
high schoolers.

Mm-hmm starts to clean up her own mess, washing her dishes and silverware. Judge puts her items in the sink while Mm-hmm is washing.

MM-HMM
Your office co-
worker didn't say
anything?

JUDGE
No.

MM-HMM
They wouldn't
because it probably
helps get the
ethnic contracts.

Judge washes her hands and face over sink, while Mm-hmm is spreading the paper down.

JUDGE
I doubt that.

MM-HMM
Who would, or could
say something to
you without you
taking it as an
ethnic slur?

Judge pauses and sits at the table again wiggling at Mm-hmm upside down paper.

JUDGE
I still think you're jealous of where I am. So, what's your excuse man-hater?

MM-HMM
I don't hate men. I just don't love them anymore.

Judge looks around for someone else. She holds up both her hands as if she's embarrassed herself.

JUDGE
Oh! OK, that's your choice who you sleep with.

Mm-hmm looks Judge.

MM-HMM
You're so lazy. Learn how to clean up behind yourself. You have a one track mind. Love and sex are two different things.

Judge nods her head sarcastically, while searching through kitchen cabinets.

MM-HMM
What are you looking for?

JUDGE
I'm looking for a violin for the bull your dishing out. Everybody's having sex. Even Uncle Walter.

MM-HMM
You just can't believe I can still live and be celibate. You just figured if I don't have a man, don't want a man, I must desire a woman. You're so shallow.

JUDGE
I guess you're so deep. I'm not intimidated by you. Men are intimidated by you. You're so animated. I'm not afraid to tell you.

Judge demonstrates Mm-hmm's demeanor and mannerism including walk. Mm-hmm gets up from the table and leaves the kitchen, on the way out she cuts the lights off.

MM-HMM
Finished your dishes counselor.

Judge jets after her, but turns and uses the sink light to finish her dishes and silverware. She runs out of kitchen.

EXT. DAY-CARE PARKING LOT-LATE AFTERNOON

Brother drives into the parking lot, and jumps out of his truck. Maria is walking toward the van with the kids in tow. He hugs the kids and hugs her and she is distant.

They work on opposite sides of the van placing both children in car seats. Brother tries to get Maria attention for a loving look. She ignores him. She walks around to driver's side. Brother steps aside and she starts van.

BROTHER
Can I talk with you for a minute?

Maria closes the doors, leans on the van and looks at him. She slides her sunglasses over her eyes. He tries to lift them off, but she taps his hand.

BROTHER
I forgot Babe.

She immediately turns toward the van to opens it but he touches her shoulder.

BROTHER
I'm sorry, there is a better explanation.

Brother starts pacing and looks at his watch. He raises his arms surrendering.

BROTHER
You say something. You know all my answers and questions.

Maria peaks over her sunglasses looking directly at Brother and not smiling.

MARIA
I'm not a single parent. I don't want to be one. We each have responsibilities, including our jobs and children. What about school? What about your customers? Have you thought about them?

Brother smacks his forehead at the mention of the above responsibilities. He nods his head.

BROTHER
I have.

Maria shifts her glasses back over her eyes and gives Brother the stop sign. He shuts up.

MARIA
You asked me to talk. I know you been doing this Uncle Walter thing and that's good, but you have enough to juggle now.

Brother's phone rings and he glances at it. Then back to Maria. He points to her motioning he has to take this. She turns to leave.

BROTHER
Hello, hello. You're breaking up. I'll call you right back.

He hangs it up. He looks at Maria for assurance but she provides none.

MARIA
Have you noticed that you didn't get a lot of calls today. I've had them forwarded to me. I have the list.

Maria opens the van door and tucks a fist full of messages in Brother's hand.

MARIA
The church also called and the sink is stopped up.

BROTHER

Really! OK, I'll take care of that before I come.

Brother looks through the messages, half way smiling at the responsibilities.

MARIA

Don't you have class tonight plus homework?

BROTHER

Perhaps tomorrow it can be taken care of.

MARIA

Honey, I have to get the kids home and pick up Tia.

BROTHER

I could pick up Tia!

Maria shakes her head no and she enters the van. Brother walks over to the passenger window. Maria slowly lowers the window. Brother waves and smiles at the kids. He offers to kiss Maria's lips but she snubs him for her cheek.

Brother's phone rings again.

BROTHER

Gillespie plumbing

Maria rolls windows up and pulls away, as Brother motions for her to wait. Brother's other phone rings as he ravages to find it. Maria rolls the window down and shouts back at Brother.

MARIA

I know how to say no.

Maria plunges the van into the evening air. Brother's family departs. He's strapped to the concrete and his hands paralyzed to his thighs as the his phones continually screams.

EXT. MM-HMM'S PORCH STEPS ANOTHER DAY

Deuce straddles the porch railing, head blending with the wood in a polished snore. Mm-hmm undo's her loud door latch and spies her morning paper. She relaxes her eyes east and west as Deuce movements persist.

MM-HMM
Deuce, wake up,
wake up what are
you doing here?

His stupor gripping. Mm-hmm's bare-feet sidesteps to him. She paper-slaps him with a newspaper and his restlessness explodes.

DEUCE
Why did you attack
me?

MM-HMM
Why are you here so
early?

Deuce scans the heavens and hoist his one hand against the sun's burst. Mm-hmm returns to the front door. Deuce drags himself inside.

INT. MM-HMM'S HOME-MOMENTS LATER

DEUCE
It's been two days.

Mm-hmm hobbles her morning body into the hallway, opens a closet and assembles a toiletry bag. Then cuts an eye toward Deuce. He lunges at her silence toward the bathroom meeting her black shower towels midway.

MM-HMM
Don't put on the same clothes.

Deuce mumbles inaudible. Mm-hmm surveys another closet and pries out taunt jeans and old tee. She plops the folded faded attire outside the bathroom's entrance.

Mm-hmm ushers herself to the kitchen fingering crud from her eye. She fills whistle pot and ignites one stove's eye. She gestures toward kitchen cabinets, but alters for the fridge. She assess the contents, shakes no and whirls around Deuce, who is fully dressed and displayed against a wall.

She gathers herself, points penetrating toward the bathroom.

DEUCE
I'm finished.

MM-HMM
Two days, two showers.

Deuce zips his mouth close and vacates the kitchen.

EXT. BELAIR FUNERAL HOME MOMENTS-LATER

Dern and Fern are transferring items inside the van from the building. They both trot while working.

DERN
I'll run this by the dumpster and come back.

Fern nods yes, then recants.

FERN
Don't go across the street.

DERN

I have to check the mail, maybe check my sandwich.

FERN

You not leaving me here, that long.

Both pause and swallow hard at what's unfolded recently. Dern goes to the mail box yanks the mail out and him and his sister lunch wrapped in newspaper, takes a bite and heads back to the van. He speaks to Fern

DERN

You think he's alive?

FERN

He wasn't on the outside when I finally got there. It was only you.

Dern continues hauling chairs and tables.

DERN

Billy said there was no bodies in there.

FERN

There two in there now. One's walking. It could have been four.

Dern ejects himself into Fern's space but she pummels his forehead with her palm. He flutters to the floor, using the van door to undo his tumble.

DERN

I just had a question.

Fern signals for the question.

DERN

What?

FERN

You and me plus that guy, and the knock behind the door. I mean who? Who was that knock behind the door

They both stand lunging forward. They hold hands and walk in building.

INT. BELAIR FUNERAL HOME-MOMENTS LATER

Fern and Dern walk lightly and whisper around the building. They enter the office where Uncle Walter ashes are. Fern sees the open vault, she slides on urn dust again.

DERN

You're a lady remember.

Fern waves him off and he laughs. They sees the open vault and are jolted and speak in unison.

FERN/DERN

Was it open?

They swallow hard steering their way around to view the contents of the vault. Dern grips his sister jacket but is primed to run out of the building first. The urn is still present.

DERN

That guy was looking . . .

He points his thumb over his back, and she points forward.

FERN

For that guy.

DERN

Maybe those guys
met up.

FERN
You know it don't
work that way.

Fern retrieves brooms and toss's one to Dern and both sweep in opposite direction heading away from the vault.

DERN
Oh well, when you
dead some people
looking down and
some looking up.

FERN
What are we going
to do about the new
guy knowing the
dead guy?

DERN
We have to look for
the new guy, who
looking for a guy
who he don't know
is a dead guy, like
the dead dust guy.

Fern rubs her head. Dern sticks his head out for rubbing but she smacks it.

FERN
Suppose we let
Billy know.

DERN
No! We let him know
and he won't pay
us.

Fern paces the floor, touching items and observing the room and snaps her finger.

FERN

We could have our own funeral for him. Once we find him. It will be fun.

Dern is spooked and jumps at any noise. He quickly steels himself.

DERN

How we going to bury him/them?

Fern stretches her hand out and surrenders the room full of coffins. They both smile.

DERN

I'm no grave digger. I have standards. I can't do all the work.

FERN

I have to supervise.

Dern lowers his head.

DERN

Those twelve years in primary school really helped. Once we find and bury the new guy, what are we going to do with the dust dude?

Fern scratches her head and clasps her chin, thinking.

FERN

We have to find the new guy to bury him with the dust guy.

They are family, right?

DERN
That's what the new guy said about the dead guy.

FERN
So family need to be with family.

DERN
Bury them together?

FERN
More than that, pour him in with him.

Dern laughs.

DERN
Isn't that what I just said?

Fern shakes her head no.

FERN
Don't talk to your supervisor like that!

INT. RESTAURANT-MIDNIGHT

Brother and other employees hover over a stove and counter. The sounds of a packed night at a restaurant summons speed. Brother cooks, while other employees wiz behind him. Brother's eyes are soaked with sleep, but he weaves trying to steady himself.

WAITER

I need two benz
with light kraut!

The waiter places a dinner ticket on a high ring, which spins. Brother snatches it off the ring and passes a plate of soup and a sandwich through a window.

BROTHER
Ready up, S. and S.

Brother extends his legs out to steady his rock. He wipes his brow. He scrambles three eggs and yanks a well-done steak off the grill.

BROTHER
Cow and chicks
Ready up.

He passes the plate through the window. Another cook signals Brother to speed up the work, but Brother throws a towel thru the window.

BROTHER
Trot your self-back
here.

WAITER
You need to quicken
it up, we're just
getting started.

BROTHER
Say that back here,
instead of talking
up front.

Another cook waves his hand at Brother. The waiter yells at Brother.

WAITER
You've been here
long enough. You
know the war.

Brother prepares food, and just looks through him.

BROTHER
Chicken on a square raft, ready up!

Another waiter shoots by and shouts out.

ANOTHER WAITER
How's my benz coming? I need a swimming twisted strings.

BROTHER
Up or down?

ANOTHER WAITER
Up stream.

Brother nods his head and pulls a pot from above his head. He snatches two precooked fish and untangles a roll of spaghetti. Brother's phone sirens. He drops the entire box of spaghetti in the heating water. He puts the phone to his shoulder.

He stumbles reaching for a set of tongs, and looks out the side window overlooking the Belair nursing and funeral home.

BROTHER
Hello, Gillespie repair.

A waiter comes in, shouts at Brother.

WAITER
Off the phone, I need the two benz light kraut.

Brother stiffens at the shout and whirls around and simultaneously drops his phone into the boiling liquid. He swings the tongs at waiter then fishes out his phone. He then stirs the spaghetti. He scrapes the toasted Reuben off the grill. The waiter leaves.

BROTHER
Light kraut benz,
ready up.

Brother audits the window of activity at the nursing and funeral home. Brother phone sizzles and he snatches it open.

BROTHER
Hello.

There is no answer. He shakes the phone and cooks.

I/E. BROTHER'S TRUCK- BELAIR PARKING LOT-DAY

Brother's writing on clipboard, shaking and wiping his phone. He checks for a signal. The truck is facing both buildings. He puts his head back, his cap over his eyes and drifts off.

Brother's phone vibrates, and he lunges forward.

BROTHER
Hello, hello. I can
hear you! Can you
hear me?

There is no response. He continually shakes it to no avail. He drops the phone on the dash, leans back dozing, and then awakens. He drags himself out of the truck, walks to the middle of both buildings and scans both directions. He walks toward the funeral home. He rubs his nose, and smells the air.

Elsie stands in the shadows of the sun behind a bush. Her cigarette smoke hangs above her head. Brother negotiates his tired body over. He leans against the wall.

ELSIE
You tired?

BROTHER
Tired and old.

ELSIE
You're only old
when you know
you're dying.

Brother pauses, and looks toward the Funeral home.

BROTHER
Why are you
outside?

ELSIE
Why aren't you
inside?

Brother points toward funeral home.

BROTHER
I was going back
inside that
building.

ELSIE
You still need to
see Walter.

BROTHER
Huh?

ELSIE
The other Walter.

Brother paces, and starts to back up and walk away from Elsie.

BROTHER
You know Miss
Elsie, I think I'd
better take my own
chances elsewhere.

Brother grasp her shoulder and turns her around toward the door she exited from. Elsie snaps her head at his hand on her shoulder and he moves his hand.

ELSIE

Don't touch me. You
young people want
to do everything
alone. You don't
need us do you?

Brother surrender his hands.

BROTHER

Its not that Miss
Elsie, I'm zapped.
I worked last
night. Uncle Walter
is coming home
tomorrow and I'd
like to meet him
before he gets. . .

ELSIE

Here, he's here,
come on he's here!

She slips thru a small door. Brother looks around as if someone observing and he stoops down and closes the door behind him.

INT. HALL BETWEEN NURSING HOME AND FUNERAL HOME-MOMENTS-LATER

Elsie uses her walker down a dim lit hallway. She is moving a little faster. Elsie points at her oxygen tank and cigarettes. Brother muster his strength to carry them. He sighs at the oxygen's stand and cigarette pack attached to the tank.

Brother follows her down a hall to a glass window. She stops and flattens her hand against the clean glass. Brother stands behind her watching her through the mirrored glass.

BROTHER

Miss Elsie, we have
to get going.

ELSIE

We're here.

Brother surveys the glass. His phone jerks a limp sound and he scrabbles for it.

BROTHER
Hello, hello. Can you hear me?

He plucks the receiver to no avail. He closes the phone.

ELSIE
Push!

Brother pushes where her hand is but nothing happens. He accidently touches her hand and she lashes a grim look at him. She touches different points on the glass, fingering each spot. Their fingerprints are all over the mirror.

BROTHER
What are we looking for?

Elsie silently mouth's Brother's words.

ELSIE
I'm taking you to see your uncle.

BROTHER
Then, why are we at a glass mirror?

ELSIE
Push!

They continue to push all over the glass. Brother sits on the floor with his back against the glass. It causes a door to open and spin around. Elsie clinks through on one side and Brother scoots through on the other.

INT. NURSING HOME RESIDENT'S ROOM-SECONDS LATER

A resident is sleeping in the bed and immediately sits up as Elsie clinks through his room followed by Brother. Elsie waves his hand at him without looking and he lays back down. She opens the outside door and peeks out, viewing the nurse's desk.

ELSIE
Just knock on that door across from here.

Brother searches her for answers.

BROTHER
I can't stand in the hallway waiting for an answer.

ELSIE
Knock and go on in. That's your uncle in there. Staff do it all the time.

BROTHER
Wouldn't it be better, if you go ahead of me.

Elsie shakes her head yes, then points to the occupants door which says no smoking. She removes the cannular from underneath her collar and inserts it in her nose, then lights her cigarette. Brother moves away from her.

BROTHER
You're flammable Miss Elsie.
She smiles. He knocks at the door and enters.

ELSIE
Thank you.

INT. WALTER'S ROOM SECONDS LATER

The room is immaculate and has earth colors. It is similar to a condo instead of a nursing home room. A man is sitting with his back to Brother typing on the computer.

WALTER
Just leave the tray on the nightstand.

Brother clears his throat and Walter turns around.

WALTER
Where's the brunch tray?

BROTHER
I'm sorry sir, I'm not. . . Are you my Uncle Walter?

He spins his computer chair and faces Brother.

WALTER
We don't look like family. There are a couple other Walters here. I can't reveal there last names, because privacy issues. You do understand?

BROTHER
I do, I've met the rest.

WALTER
So, I guess that makes me your uncle, huh?

Brother smiles and offers his hand. Walter walks over and they exchange handshakes. There is an awkward silence.

WALTER

What's your name?
Nephew.

BROTHER
Brother.

Walter shakes his head.

WALTER
I guess you have a
sister and her name
is sister?

He chuckles at his own humor. Brother is strait faced. Brother inventories the room. Walter watches him.

BROTHER
Are you almost
packed?

Walter turns back to his computer and adjust something and saves, then turns off computer screen.

WALTER
Actually, I need to
unpack.

Brother returns his focus on Walter.

BROTHER
You're going with
us tomorrow.

WALTER
I just got here.

Brother goes over to the window and lifts up the blinds and the sun shines into the room.

BROTHER
You just arrived? I
thought you were
ready to leave.

WALTER

How old are you Brother?

BROTHER
I'm in my early thirties.

The bald Walter stands and walks into a closet and comes out with a toupee, which makes him looks twenty years younger.

WALTER
I'm in my early forties. I suppose your uncle is a lot older?

Brother nods shakes his hand and pauses at the door.

BROTHER
Walter, why are you here? You're not old, in a traditional way?

Walter laughs.

WALTER
Who do you work for? Do you work for Uncle Sam?

BROTHER
A deli and I'm self-employed plumber.

He peeks around his own room as if checking for microphones.

WALTER
100% disability. Agent Orange offspring. No family nowhere. I'm old because they know I'm dying.

Dejected, Brother shakes Walter’s hand again and he exits.

EXT. FUNERAL HOME DAY-LATER

Brother walks around the outside of the darken windows, trying to glimpse in. He wipes off some of the dust. He taps at each window around the building. He untangles some ivy from the mammoth front door. He knocks.

INT. FUNERAL HOME-MOMENTS-LATER

Dern and Fern jump from window to window at each sound. They stand in the middle of the room back to back as the sound surrounds them. They whisper.

DERN
What do you think
it is?

He grabs his sister's hand for comfort. She peels his hand free from hers. The knocking from the front door continues. Both inch themselves to inspect the door.

They drop to the floor and look underneath the door and watch the movements. They grapple with who will inspect the peephole. Fern yields and slides up and looks out, then drops back to the floor.

FERN
Couldn't see them
completely.

DERN
How many was it?

The knocks get louder.

Dern gives her a thumbs up sign and Fern hesitates but looks again. She drops to the floor again. She stares stoically. Dern looks at her and nudges her. His arms are wide open expecting an answer.

FERN
It’s the dead guy!

DERN
Why is a dead guy knocking?

Dern gets on all fours crawls toward another door. Fern stoops down and follows him.

EXT. FUNERAL HOME MOMENTS-LATER

Brother listens to the door.

BROTHER
I hear your voices.

He bangs harder and kicks at the metal door.

INT. FUNERAL HOME-MOMENTS-LATER

The twins remain on all fours, but turn and crawl back to the door. Fern stands behind the door, with a white sheet. Dern to the right of the door grabs a candlestick holder. Dern nods to Fern as she unlocks the door and it squeaks open.

I/E. FUNERAL HOME DOORWAY SECONDS-LATER

The door opens and Brother freezes. Dern and Fern lunge to open space. Fern shoves the white sheet over her brother and Dern hits his sister in the head with the candlestick holder. They both drop as Brother enters and offers a hand.

BROTHER
Why are you fighting?

They observe him from the floor. They look at each other. Fern rubbing her head and Dern untangles himself from blanket.

BROTHER

Does my Uncle
Walter work here?

DERN

He doesn't work
here, he's retired.

Fern needles Dern to shut up. He winces.

BROTHER

Where do I find
him? He's going
home tomorrow.

They both stand up.

FERN

You could pick him
up today.

Brother startled. His phone wails and it startles them. He tries to answer it. Shaking it and walking around for reception.

BROTHER

Hello, I can hear
you. Can you hear
me?

Brother shakes his head.

DERN

Nice phone.

Brother scours at Dern. He closes his phone.

BROTHER

I can't pick him up
today. Everything
is scheduled for
tomorrow. I do need
to talk with him.

Fern pulls Dern over by his sleeve and his foot gets caught in the blanket. He falls again. She whispers to her Brother.

FERN
What are we going to do?

Fern snaps her finger at the thought of an idea. They motion for Brother to give them five minutes. They back out the room. Brother moves forward as they move backward. They turn and zip into the office.

They spring to the phone together one dials the other is at the receiver. They scatter items on the desk skimming for Bill-lee's number. Brother follows them but their backs are to him.

Brother tiptoes in and sidesteps papers. Brother's foot slides on some dust and he catches himself on the open door vault. Fern and Dern shiver at the sudden noise. They see his hand. Fern scampers over Brother's touching the vault door.

DERN
If you could wait outside sir, we'll be just a minute.

Fern tries to slowly close the door, but Brother won't release it. She smiles.

FERN
Yes, we must get permission from our superior.

Brother releases the door and Fern slowly tries to close it. Brother walks past her toward Dern and she freezes. Brother glances at the contents of the vault and barely sees Gillespie.

BROTHER

Wait a second.

He turns back and opens the vault and sees Uncle Walter's first name and last name. Fern tries to block him but he scours at her. She drifts away. Brother fingers the year 1999 and methodically picks up the urn.

He commandeers the urn with vise-grip hands. He holds it toward them. Fern nods yes and Dern looks away. Brother drops to his knees and Dern rolls a chair over. Brother leans on it, hyperventilates and cries. His phone rings and he vomits.

INT. BANK OFFICE-DAY

Brother hands the office manager paperwork, they shake hands and he escorts Brother into private viewing room. A curtain is drawn.

INT. BANK SAFE DEPOSIT BOX VIEWING ROOM-MOMENTS LATER

Brother wipes his face from tears. He inserts a key-card, which opens the box. An ageing blue satchel has several hundred pictures, an 8-track cassette, a make-shift album cover with an orange vinyl record. Brother replaces all in the safe deposit box and departs.

EXT. BROTHERS HOUSE FRONT PORCH-AFTERNOON

Brother's rocking in a chair and watching cars go by. Brakes assault his driveway as Mm-hmm, Deuce, Comesee, and Judge appear exhaling with anticipation.

DEUCE

Where is he?

Brother points inside the house, Mm-hmm questions.

MM-HMM

Your house is so
big, where inside?

Brother stands and follows them as other family members arrive and hijack street parking places and penetrate Brothers domain. Family voices are shouting through the house.

COMESEE
Uncle Walter, Uncle
Walter.

Judge sits down breathless from running the stairs. Comesee kids have gone to their cousins rooms. Others are in kitchen with Maria.

COMESEE
Which room Brother?

Brother finally enters and shouts out.

BROTHER
Everybody in the
family room.

They file in the room facing the fireplace. Brother paces over and stand in front of the fireplace.

DEUCE
We're not hear for
none of your
lectures, just tell
us where Uncle
Walter is.

Brother salutes Deuce. Deuce holds his hand expecting a rebuttal. Brother arms are stretched across the mantel above the fireplace. Brother raises his hands to quiet the people down.

BROTHER
Uncle Walter is here but before he shows up, he wanted me to share some things from the safe deposit box.

Brother whips the satchel off the mantel. He turns it up side down in the air and holding to the cassette and album, he lets all the photos flicker to the floor. The family tumble over each other, looking at photos.

There are pictures of Uncle Walter, his brothers, which are their uncles and fathers. Mostly of when everyone were children. Uncle Walter has pictures of him meeting celebrities and dignitaries of local and other countries.

BROTHER
I've made copies for everyone, they're collectables.

Brother holds up the 8-track cassette and orange vinyl album. A younger family member speaks.

YOUNGSTER
What are those things Uncle Brother?

BROTHER
It’s something people use to play music on.

He holds up the album cover, which has writing on it in a circle. A younger family member reads the album cover aloud.

YOUNGSTER
The sound track of my life by Walter Gillespie.

Brother raises it up.

BROTHER
Does anyone have anything to play it on?

No one raises their hands. Comesee speaks.

JUDGE
I appreciate the dramatics but I do have to go. Where's Uncle Walter so we can thank him?

Brother lowers his head then raises it.

BROTHER
Just one more thing!

There is a general sigh in the room, followed by murmuring.

BROTHER
We do have a consensus that we will take Uncle Walter on a monthly basis.

DEUCE
I ain't doing no census. They have to find me. They use that stuff to control your mind. It’s like a drug.

Everyone scans Deuce who blushes and lightly scratches himself. Brother throws his arms up for attention. Brother put his arm on the mantel and rises the urn, then lowers it chest high.

BROTHER

This is Uncle
Walter.

The family falls deadly silent, most look at each other and at some the pictures. They measure Brother's face for laughter. Some begin to laugh, but Brother remains serious.

JUDGE
That's not what I
think it is. Is it?

Brother shoves it toward Mm-hmm but, she pushes it away, lightly brushing her skirt. Brother offers the urn to everyone and everyone refuses.

JUDGE
How long has he
been dead?

Brother smacks his forehead and paces.

BROTHER
He's been dead
since 1999.

DEUCE
The dude has been
gone ten years.
Where's he been?

Brother puts his arm around Deuce.

BROTHER
Hey cuz, the
pictures tell us a
lot.

COMESEE
The 8-track and
album will tell us
more. Whose has
one?

Everyone looks around at each other.

DEUCE
I don't even know
where to steal one

if I did, it may
not work.

BROTHER
I know where to go.

INT. BELAIR NURSING HOME DAYROOM-DAY

The entire Gillespie family and the senior citizens are listening to Uncle Walter orange album. The room is filled with jazz, rock and roll, classical, country, and many international songs. Brother stands searching for Elsie.

Carmen turns the record off and inserts the eight track in a donated player. She presses the shift button and it won't work. The sound is muffled. Everyone has enjoyed the music and the seniors file back to their rooms.

The Gillespie group waves goodbye and stand at the door, reluctant to leave. Brother sees smoke and hears a squeaky wheel approaching from around a corner.

BROTHER
Wait a minute. I
want everyone to
meet Elsie.

Elsie emerges from the sun-dimmed hallway. She approaches the family.

ELSIE
Did you find him? I
was right, wasn't
I?

Brother attempts to hug her, but doesn't. The family comes over and marvels at her. They back off a little because of her combination of oxygen and cigarettes.

BROTHER

You, were right
Miss Elsie, he was
here. It's good
seeing you again.

ELSIE
I heard the music.
I was just getting
here. Where's
everybody going?
Is this your Uncle
family? Where's
your uncle.

Brother stoops down on one knee so he's level with Elsie. She smiles and he looks in her eyes. He touches her oxygen stand. She doesn't react.

BROTHER
Uncle Walter passed
on, some time ago.

The family comes nearer as Elsie is suddenly quiet. She searches their faces.

JUDGE
We came here to
celebrate his life
with those who may
have knew what he
loved.

ELSIE
I'm sorry,
everybody was
suppose to take him
home, yes?

MM-HMM
Actually, it would
have been
yesterday.

COMESEE
We were ready.

Elsie looks at Deuce who is starting to nod out.

ELSIE

Take me! Please take me. You said everybody was ready. I stay ready, so I won't have to get ready.

Elsie touches Brother's sleeve, which catches his attention. Brother scans back at the Gillespie family.

ELSIE

Do you think I'll fit in?

The eight track cassette player starts to play a tune by the Beetles called, "Hey Jude".

THE END

www.ingramcontent.com/pod-product-compliance
Lightning Source LLC
Chambersburg PA
CBHW052341100426
42736CB00047B/3405

* 9 7 8 1 9 4 8 8 2 9 9 4 6 *